Dedicated to the memory of Nicholas Fodor

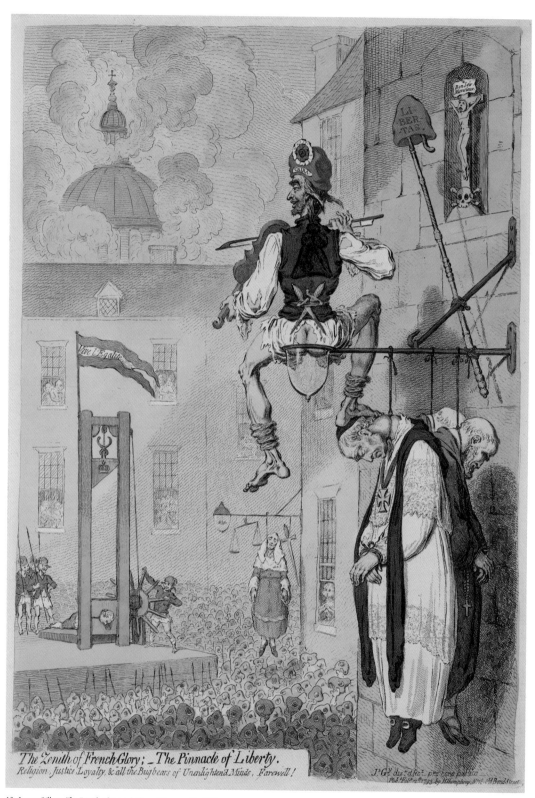

13 James Gillray, *The Zenith of French Glory*, February 12, 1793

Face à Face

FRENCH AND ENGLISH
CARICATURES OF THE FRENCH REVOLUTION
AND ITS AFTERMATH

James A. Leith and Andrea Joyce

THIS EXHIBITION IS ORGANIZED AND CIRCULATED BY

THE ART GALLERY OF ONTARIO WITH THE GENEROUS SUPPORT OF

THE TRIER-FODOR FOUNDATION

ART GALLERY OF ONTARIO

MUSEE DES BEAUX-ARTS DE L'ONTARIO

TORONTO, ONTARIO

The purchase of the majority of the works in this exhibition and the exhibition itself have been made possible by the Trier-Fodor Foundation.

Copyright © 1989 by the Art Gallery of Ontario

All rights reserved

ISBN 0-919777-71-6

The Art Gallery of Ontario is generously funded by the Ontario Ministry of Culture and Communications. Additional financial support is received from the Municipality of Metropolitan Toronto – Cultural Affairs Division, Communications Canada, and the Canada Council.

Canadian Cataloguing in Publication Data

Leith, James A., 1931-

    Face à face : French and English caricatures of the French Revolution and its aftermath

Catalogue to an exhibition organized by the Art Gallery of Ontario and held at Musée du Québec, Jan. 26-Mar. 12, 1989, Art Gallery of Ontario, July 14-Sept. 10, 1989, and Winnipeg Art Gallery, Oct. 28-Dec. 10, 1989.

Bibliography: p.

ISBN 0-919777-71-6

1. France – History – Revolution, 1789-1799 – Caricatures and cartoons – Exhibitions. 2. France – History – Consulate and Empire, 1799-1815 – Caricatures and cartoons – Exhibitions. 3. Caricatures and cartoons – France – Exhibitions. 4. Caricatures and cartoons – England – Exhibitions. 5. French wit and humor, Pictorial – Exhibitions. 6. English wit and humor, Pictorial – Exhibitions. I. Joyce, Andrea, 1964- . II. Art Gallery of Ontario. III. Musée du Québec. IV. Winnipeg Art Gallery. V. Title.

DC149.5.L45 1989   741.5′9′0740113541

C89-093220-4

Itinerary of the Exhibition

Please note that venues and dates are subject to change.

Musée du Québec, Quebec City
January 26 – March 12, 1989

Art Gallery of Ontario, Toronto
July 14 – September 10, 1989

Winnipeg Art Gallery, Manitoba
October 28 – December 10, 1989

Editor: Vivian Elias
Graphic Design: Marilyn Bouma-Pyper
Photography: Photographic Services, Art Gallery of Ontario
Photocomposition: Crocker Bryant Inc.
Printing: MacKinnon-Moncur Ltd., Printers and Lithographers

Cover : 67 Anonymous, *Serment des Calicots*, c.August 1817

TABLE OF CONTENTS

St James's Street.

HUMPHREY

VERY SLIPPY-WEATHER.

PREFACE

35 James Gillray, *Very Slippy Weather*, February 10, 1808

SINCE THE TIME OF WILLIAM THE CONQUEROR, THE ENGLISH AND French, facing each other across the English Channel, have been alternately threatened, challenged, and fascinated by each other. Never have these sentiments been more graphically portrayed than in the satirical prints produced by the two nations during the French Revolution and its aftermath. Given the special interest that this theme holds for French and English Canadians, we are especially pleased to have the Musée du Québec and the Winnipeg Art Gallery as partners in this venture, and to see this exhibition hung as a pendant at each centre to *A Picture of the French Revolution*, organized by Claudette Hould, of the Université du Québec à Montréal.

This exhibition has been put together to mark the two hundredth anniversary of the storming of the Bastille on July 14, 1789. It is the first to be drawn almost exclusively from the collection of caricatures formed at the Art Gallery of Ontario since 1976 by Dr. Katharine Lochnan, Curator of Prints and Drawings, with funds provided by the Trier-Fodor Foundation. This ongoing special fund, which makes possible the purchase and exhibition of "humorous, satirical and illustrative graphic art" was established to set the work of the artist and illustrator Walter Trier (1890-1951) in context, and reflect his debt to, and love of, the history of caricature. Given the size of the collection, which now numbers over 300 sheets, and the speed with which it has been growing, this is but the first of many exhibitions that will be generated from the Trier-Fodor collection in years to come.

We are very much in the debt of the Trier and Fodor families, and would like to take this opportunity to express our deep thanks for their ongoing interest and support, to the artist's widow Helen Trier, their daughter Gretl and her late husband Nicholas Fodor; as well as the Fodors' daughter Emily, son Joseph, and his wife Jill. Their imagination, vision and enthusiasm are reflected in this area of the Prints and Drawings programme.

I would also like to thank the authors of the catalogue, Professor James Leith of Queen's University in Kingston, Ontario, and Andrea Joyce of Toronto, who began her research as a summer student in the Prints and Drawings department. On behalf of Andrea Joyce, I would like to thank Larry Pfaff and the Art Gallery of Ontario Reference Library staff; Maia-Mari Sutnik and Faye Van Horne in Photographic Services; Catherine Van Baren, who read the first drafts of the entries; Catherine Dunets, who made sense of the word processor; and Lucille Le Blanc and Wendy Hebditch, who typed the manuscript. Thanks must also go to Susan Johnson for the print on loan to the Art Gallery of Ontario that was used for didactic purposes in this exhibition; Alan Suddon and Mary Holford, who helped to date the caricatures by identifying fashion trends; David Bindman at the University of London, who contributed information on the history of caricature; McAllister Johnson, at the University of Toronto, who advised on the organization of bibliographic material; and Douglas Joyce, who proofread the entries. Dr. Johnson and Dr. Joyce were both helpful in identifying the subject matter in many of the caricatures and their effort and enthusiasm are appreciated. Special mention goes to Brenda Rix, whose catalogue of Rowlandson caricatures, *Our Old Friend Rolly: Watercolours, Prints, and Book Illustrations by Thomas Rowlandson in the Collection of the Art Gallery of Ontario*, set the standard for this catalogue.

Thanks also to Dr. Katharine Lochnan, Curator of Prints and Drawings, who conceived the idea of the exhibition, and to a number of staff members of the Art Gallery of Ontario who have been involved in bringing it to fruition: Michael Parke-Taylor, Assistant Curator of Prints and Drawings; Glenda Milrod, Head of Extension Services; Alan Terakawa, Head of Publications and Design; Vivian Elias, Editor; and Marilyn Bouma-Pyper, Designer.

William J. Withrow, Director

FOREWORD

THE TRIER-FODOR FOUNDATION FUND FOR THE PURCHASE AND EXHIBItion of "humorous, satirical and representational graphic art," established in 1976, has made possible the purchase during the past twelve years of over 300 prints, drawings, and watercolours from the sixteenth to the twentieth centuries. We hope in time to build a collection that will provide a comprehensive survey of the history of caricature of all periods and schools.

While our initial thrust has been to secure outstanding works that represent the major figures in the history of caricature, we have also begun to develop some areas in depth. Since caricature enjoyed a "golden age" in Britain during the last half of the eighteenth century, and in France during the first half of the nineteenth, the collection is strongest in this area. While our purchase decisions are dictated more by aesthetic than documentary concerns, the relatively strong representation of caricatures of the French as seen by the English during the period of the French Revolution, and of the English viewed through the eyes of the French after they began to travel in France at the end of the Napoleonic Wars, has given rise to this exhibition.

The history of caricature is a vast, largely uncharted, field and it was necessary for the Gallery to determine on what basis to select works that would act as a complement to a fine art collection containing original prints, drawings, and watercolours. Most caricature collections are found in libraries where they complement books and archival material. We decided that we would only collect prints which were themselves good impressions in good condition, which were hand-coloured at the time of their creation, and which were stylistically and conceptually innovative. In this, we have been greatly aided by the advice of the foremost specialist and dealer in the field, Andrew Edmunds of London, England. The majority of the English works in the exhibition were acquired from Edmunds, and the French works from Arsène Bonafous-Murat in Paris.

This is the first exhibition to be pulled almost exclusively from the Trier-Fodor collection at the Gallery. Because of the rarity of caricatures made in France during the Revolution, we have borrowed a handful of prints from the collection of David Bindman, Professor of Art History at Westfield College, University of London. Professor Bindman is concurrently organizing an exhibition of caricatures of the French Revolution for the British Museum, which will take place in 1989. We are very grateful to him for lending us these works. We are also grateful to the late Jack Johnson and to Gilbert Bagnani for gifts that are included in the exhibition.

Katharine Lochnan, Curator of Prints and Drawings

Lord-gueil   *Lady-scorde.*

A Paris, chez Basset rue St Jacques N°64.   Dép.é à la D.on

HISTORICAL INTRODUCTION

by James A. Leith

73 Anonymous (French), *Lord-gueil Lady-scorde,*
April 27, 1819

THIS EXHIBITION DEALS MAINLY WITH HOW TWO MAJOR EUROPEAN powers, England and France, viewed each other in caricatures in the age of the French Revolution, the Empire, and the Restoration. These two countries face each other across a long channel which at its narrowest point, between Dover and the Cap Gris-Nez, is only twenty-one miles wide. The two countries, however, cannot even agree on the name of this channel, the English calling it the English Channel, as though it were theirs, and the French labelling it *la Manche,* meaning "the Sleeve." The two countries differ not only in their languages but in the roots of those languages. Despite the infusion of French words after the Norman Conquest, English is basically a Germanic tongue, while French is derived from Latin, giving it affinities to Italian, Spanish, and Portuguese. They differ too in the history of their religions: England had broken with the Roman Catholic Church in the sixteenth century, while France remained a predominantly Catholic country. The Protestant minority in France had enjoyed a small degree of toleration in the seventeenth century under the Edict of Nantes until its revocation by Louis XIV in 1685. Four years later the English parliament passed the Toleration Act, allowing most sects to worship freely. Catholics were not included, but in fact were largely left alone.

On the eve of the French Revolution the two countries had very different political cultures. Following the rebellion known as the Fronde in the mid-seventeenth century, Louis XIV strengthened the French monarchy: he domesticated the great nobles at his imposing palace at Versailles, made government ministers subject to his will alone, used intendants to enforce his authority in the provinces, tamed the *Parlements* or high courts, and created the largest army in Europe. Some provincial representative bodies survived in a few provinces, but the central assembly, the Estates General, did not meet in the one hundred and seventy-five years before 1789. In eighteenth-century France the king in theory decided all public policies; nevertheless a politics of contestation was beginning to emerge with arguments over religious issues, taxation, the authority of the courts, and other matters occurring in pamphlets, remonstrances of the courts, and French-language newspapers published abroad. This politics of contestation could not develop completely until Louis XVI was forced by bankruptcy to summon the Estates General. In contrast, the revolutions in England in the previous century, especially the Glorious Revolution of 1688, had left parliament with extensive power and the English people with considerable freedom to debate public issues.

ENGLISH BARRACKS

These two powers, with their very different languages, religious conditions, and political cultures were also traditional enemies. Between 1689, when France declared war on England, and 1815, the year of Napoleon's final defeat at Waterloo, the two countries fought seven separate wars, which some historians have labelled collectively the Second Hundred Years' War, although the wars stretched well over a hundred years.[1] None of these seven wars was a duel between England and France alone, because in each of them at least one other European power was involved. Moreover, since these two powers each had possessions and interests in many parts of the world, the conflict was not limited to Europe. Wherever the two countries and their allies were in contact with each other – in the Caribbean, North America, the west coast of Africa, or India – there was conflict between the English and the French. At times the conflicts resembled the world wars of the twentieth century.

Such an extensive and prolonged conflict could only have been the result

11 Thomas Rowlandson, *English Barracks,* August 12, 1791

[1] Arthur Howland Buffington, *The Second Hundred Years War 1689-1815* (New York: Holt, 1929).

FRENCH BARRACKS.

12 Thomas Rowlandson, *French Barracks*, August 12, 1791

of powerful, long-lasting causes. Throughout the seven wars there were two fundamental broad areas of rivalry: one involving the relations of England with the Continent and the overall balance of power, the other involving commercial activity and colonial competition. Sometimes one area of conflict was more important, sometimes the other, but in each war both were present. In the early modern period England and France had developed characteristic sets of policies and interests. After she was excluded from the continent in the first Hundred Years' War, England turned to commercial and colonial expansion. Her power rested mainly on her navy. On the other hand, France became the most powerful continental state, having defeated the Hapsburgs by the mid-seventeenth century. Her main source of strength lay in her land army. When, however, France began to rival England in commercial and colonial expansion and to threaten English security by domination of the continent, England felt compelled to check her.

Both countries had vigorous but different cultures. From the reign of Louis XIV, 1643-1715, France led cultural developments in Europe. Her literature was widely admired and her language was used by many educated people in other countries. France was the heartland of the Enlightenment, the eighteenth-century movement to popularize a rationalistic and scientific approach to religious, social, political, and economic matters. The works of Montesquieu, Voltaire, Rousseau, and Diderot were known throughout Europe. England too experienced a flowering of literature, philosophy, and science in the seventeenth century. Francis Bacon pioneered in the development of an empirical scientific view of the world. Locke's ideas on how the mind is shaped by external sensations had great influence in France and other countries. Newton's account of how gravitation controls the movement of heavenly bodies had repercussions throughout Europe. Then in the eighteenth century England experienced a mushrooming of new literary forms – the newspaper, the periodical, the novel, and the essay. Perhaps overall French authors were better known in other countries, but England could boast of great authors such as Defoe, Swift, Pope, Richardson, Fielding, Sterne, and Goldsmith.

Despite their differences, in fact partly because of them, the educated classes of the two countries were interested in each other. Moreover, there was a lot of cross-fertilization. Bacon, Locke, and Newton had great influence on the French Enlightenment and Diderot's monumental *Encyclopédie* began as a translation of an English encyclopedia by Ephraim Chambers. English deists like Toland, Woolston, Tindal, and Middleton had a formative influence on many eighteenth-century French thinkers. Such intellectuals as Montesquieu and Voltaire visited England and later used their observations of parliament and religious diversity to criticize French absolutism and religious intolerance. In the other direction, the great French writers were known in England through the originals or translations of their works. The well-to-do English included Paris in their grand tours of European sites. Knowledge of a neighbouring country, however, does not necessarily breed understanding; sometimes it feeds or confirms prejudices. English caricaturists often lampooned French aristocrats as decadent fops, while the French often ridiculed the visiting English as unsophisticated boors.

In caricature England had a clear edge over France. Modern caricature was born in the particular circumstances that existed in England during the last third of the eighteenth century. Caricature gets its name from the Italian verb *caricare*, which means to load or to charge. A caricature is a supercharged image, one that exaggerates in order to make the subject ludicrous. It resulted from the combination of the tradition of emblematic art, bearing a political or religious message, and the Italian tradition of grotesque images. This fusion took place and flourished because of the convergence of a number of circumstances in England during the reign of George III, 1760-1820. Artists at the time enjoyed a remarkable degree of freedom in England because images were less subject to legal restrictions than written works. At the same time there was an upper class of aristocrats and merchants with money to spend on social and political satires. Moreover, the politics of the period, with the king's more active role in government, the struggles in parliament between rival factions, and a succession of great issues – the end of the Seven Years' War, the American War of Independence, the French Revolution, the Revolutionary wars, the Napoleonic domination of Europe – provided exceptional stimulation for satirists. These factors, combined with a succession of outstanding artists, like Gillray, the Cruikshanks, and Rowlandson, produced what has been called "the golden age of English caricature."[2]

In France caricature did not enjoy such favourable conditions until the very eve of the Revolution. An absolute monarchy, even one with sometimes ineffective controls, was not conducive to a flowering of graphic satire. One could not display engravings lampooning the royal family and government ministers in shop windows in Paris as one could in London. There were occasions when a considerable amount of graphic satire was produced, as at the time of the campaign by the *Parlements* and their allies against the Jesuits in the 1760s, but the fact that these were produced anonymously and clandestinely demonstrates the nature of the political system. Only as the monarchy entered its final crisis, and contestational politics developed further, were conditions favourable for the production of caricatures. Then with the meeting of the Estates General in May 1789, its transformation into the National (Constituent) Assembly in June, and the insurrections of July and August in town and country, a new political culture emerged with a large section of the population involved in politics. The advent of this new political culture produced a flood of pamphlets, newspapers, and caricatures.

The coming of the French Revolution once again created great differences between France and England and eventually produced a renewal of their old military struggle. We use the term *the* French Revolution for convenience, whereas in fact it was a series of interrelated but different events – insurrections, purges, coups, and reactions. France went in a decade from constitutional monarchy, through a moderate republic, the revolutionary dictatorship of the Committee of Public Safety, the reaction that followed the overthrow of Robespierre and his associates, the conservative Directory, and finally the Consulate dominated by Napoleon. It went too from nationalization of the church, through dechristianization, the resurgence of Catholicism, to the Corcordat of 1801 between church

[2] Michel Jouve, *L'Age d'Or de la Caricature Anglaise* (Paris: Presses de la Fondation nationale des sciences politiques, 1983).

and state. People responded to the various stages in different ways, approving of one stage of the Revolution, but unable to stomach another. To a large extent these differences in response can be traced to various answers to the question, "How much violence is justifiable in the attempt to create a new social order?"

At first the politically conscious members of the English public reacted favourably to the French Revolution, judging by comments in English newspapers and caricatures. Since the seventeenth century the English had looked on France as the homeland of tyranny; consequently they believed that the French Revolutionaries were engaged in a struggle against oppression. This approval continued until the summer of 1790, then a rift in English opinion occurred. In October of that year Edmund Burke published a pamphlet entitled *Reflections on the French Revolution*. He called attention to the evils in the movement and predicted that further excesses were to come. Seldom has a pamphlet had such an impact. Mild approval for the French Revolution gradually gave way to aversion and horror. The change altered the balance of parties in parliament, killed the possibility of reform whether moderate or revolutionary for a generation, and prepared public opinion for eventual renewal of war with France. The Whigs, the ruling party, split into those led by Fox who still sympathized with the Revolution and those who shared the fears articulated by Burke. The younger Pitt played on these fears, winning over enough Whigs to form a

fig. 1

Anonymous, *Reveil du Tiers Etat,* c.1789; Coll. de Vinck 1673, engraving and etching, 20.7 x 24.5 cm. By permission of the Bibliothèque Nationale, Paris.

fig. 2

Anonymous, *Le Joli Moine Profitant de l'occasion,* c.1790; Coll. de Vinck 3362, engraving, 18.5 x 24.8 cm. By permission of the Bibliothèque Nationale, Paris.

Le Joli Moine
Profitant de l'occasion

61 Anonymous (French), *Progrès des Lumières*, c.1820

Tory ministry in 1792. His ministries lasted until 1806. This alteration in English politics was the result of steady radicalization of the Revolution across the Channel.

At first the Revolution seemed to promise harmony among the three Estates or orders in French society – the First Estate, or clergy; the Second Estate, or nobility; and the Third Estate, or commoners, who made up the bulk of the population. When parts of the other Estates joined the Third Estate to form the National Assembly, French artists showed a representative of each Estate playing musical instruments together, dancing together, or enclosed in an equilateral triangle. The latter was a traditional symbol for the Trinity, three equal persons who constituted one God. When used to frame a representative from each Estate it symbolized the hope that they had merged into one nation. Such hoped-for unity was short-lived. Boyer de Nîmes, who in 1792 published what was perhaps the first history of caricatures, argued that caricatures had played an important role in exciting opposition to both the clergy and the aristocracy.[3] He pointed to a caricature, *Reveil du Tiers Etat* (Awakening of the Third Estate) (fig. 1), that depicted a commoner waking up and realizing that his chains had been broken. Immediately he seizes a firearm. An abbot and a noble flee from him. In the background one sees the Bastille being demolished.

The Revolution soon alienated many of the clergy. The Revolutionaries abolished religious orders because they considered monastic life socially useless and monastic vows a violation of individual freedom. This produced a spate of amusing caricatures showing monks purchasing secular clothing and dallying with former nuns. In one such caricature, *Le Joli Moine Profitant de l'occasion* (fig. 2), a shop sign announces, "Here one

3 Jacques-Marie Boyer-Brun (Boyer de Nîmes), *Histoire des caricatures de la révolte des Français...*, 2 vols (Paris, 1792). The first volume deals with revolutionary satires, the second with counter-revolutionary ones.

LA BRILLANTE TOILLETE DE LA DÉESSE DU GOUT

Qu'elle félicité pour ce jeune amoureux.   Puis qu'il peut sans rougir observer tour à tour
Il est dans ce moment au comble de ses vœux   Ces trésors enchanteurs, destinez à l'amour.

1 Anonymous (French), *La Brillante Toillete de la Déesse du Gout*, c.1770

secularizes quickly." Soon, however, the situation grew serious. In its attempt to alleviate the financial problems of the government, the Constituent Assembly nationalized church property and then proceeded to reform the church itself. The Civil Constitution of the Clergy in 1790 made priests into civil servants, elected by the citizens like other officials and paid by the state. Priests could give only nominal recognition of leadership to the Pope. Only about half the clergy were willing to swear to support this settlement, leaving the other half opposed to the Revolution. Persecution of the non-juring clergy became increasingly severe. Meanwhile the Revolution produced a cult with substitutes for Christian components – altars, creeds, hymns, sacred symbols, goddesses, and martyrs. By the fall of 1793 a dechristianization movement erupted. The attack on the non-juring clergy, and then on Christianity itself, alarmed many Europeans, including many people in England.

At the same time the Revolution turned on aristocracy. This was partly the result of the fact that many aristocrats rejected the Revolution and the loss of their privileges, some of them fleeing the country and then lobbying for foreign powers to intervene in order to crush the Revolution. The clash was also the result of the Revolutionary principle that all men are created equal and that social distinctions are justified only on the basis of social utility. Bourgeois leaders realized that they could get popular support by attacking aristocrats. In June 1790, the National Assembly suppressed titles and coats-of-arms. There was then a concerted effort to eradicate all symbols of aristocratic status on carriages, weathervanes, gates, and statues. Even the word *château* was banned. In the end the word *aristocrate* became synonymous with opposition to the Revolution. This assault on the aristocracy naturally alarmed the ruling class in England, which was composed of aristocrats, landed gentry, and merchants. This was the section of the population that could afford copper-plate satires.

The treatment of Louis XVI and of the queen also aroused opposition in England and other countries. At first it seemed that Louis could become the Father of the People, and French artists designed engravings and monuments honouring him as liberator of his subjects, but he could not wholeheartedly support the Revolution. It demolished the hierarchical social structure of which he was the apex as the chief Noble of the Sword. After the march of the market women to Versailles in October 1789, which forced the royal family to return to Paris, he was virtually a prisoner in his own capital. Moreover, he could not accept the Civil Constitution of the Clergy. His attempted flight from the country in June 1791 undermined trust in him even further. Finally the outbreak of war with Austria and Prussia in April 1792, in which he and his Austrian queen appeared to sympathize with the enemy, finished the monarchy. His subsequent trial

A Versaille a Versaille. du 5. Octobre 1789.

8 Anonymous (French), *A Versaille à Versaille*, October 1789

and execution, an act that combined regicide and patricide, outraged many English citizens, forgetting that England had executed a king in the previous century. In 1793 James Gillray satirized the execution in *The Zenith of French Glory* (cat. no. 13), which shows a bare-bottomed *sans-culotte*, bloody daggers stuck in his belt, fiddling atop a lamp standard while he watches the guillotine about to fall on the king's neck.[4] Bodies of a judge, a priest, and monks hang from the lamp standards. "Religion, Justice, Loyalty, and all the Bugbears of Unenlightened Minds, Farewell!" the artist wrote underneath.

It was the outbreak of war in April 1792 that eventually led to a complete rupture between England and France. The fighting began between France on the one hand and Austria and Prussia on the other. A number of lesser states entered the conflict with France. England did not enter the conflict until February 1793, but it was England that organized the First Coalition, one of a series of alliances organized against Revolutionary France and later Napoleonic France. This first alliance included Austria, Prussia, Russia, Spain, Portugal, Sardinia, the Two Sicilies, and four German states, including Hanover which belonged to George III. The various combatants had different objectives, but they shared two main goals: to save European civilization as it was understood by the ruling classes; and to restore the law

4 For *sans-culottes*, see p. 13.

10

Triomphe de l'Armée Parisienne réunis au Peuple a son retour de Versailles a Paris le 6 Octobre 1789

9 Anonymous (French), *Triomphe de l'Armée Parisienne réunis au Peuple a son retour de Versailles à Paris le 6 octobre 1789,* October 1789

of nations, that is, to return France to its original borders. In addition England feared French domination of the Lowlands and coveted French colonies. England was, therefore, a key player in the subsequent twenty-two years of struggle against France, sometimes alone, most often in a coalition. English caricaturists, at times subsidized by the government, helped to consolidate opinion in support of the war effort.

In this long struggle French Revolutionaries and English artists often viewed the same phenomenon differently. A good example is the decapitating machine known as the guillotine, which we have already mentioned in regard to the execution of the king.[5] This instrument consisted of two tall posts surmounted by a crossbeam. The posts were grooved so as to allow a slanted blade, heavily weighted at the top, to be raised up to the crossbeam. When released the heavy blade dropped swiftly and forcefully on the neck of the condemned person who was clamped in place by stocks. It is paradoxical that this machine, which is associated in the minds of many people with one of the most gruesome aspects of the Revolution, was in fact seen by its proponents as a contribution to human progress. Since it was a carefully designed device, tested on animals and cadavers before use, it was an example of the applied science of the age. It was also intended to be much quicker and less painful than methods of execution under the Old Regime such as breaking the person on the wheel and burning the mutilated body alive. Moreover, all those condemned would be executed on the

5 A. Kershaw, *A History of the Guillotine* (London, 1865) provides a good brief history of the machine.

same machine, and since decapitation had been reserved for aristocrats, the guillotine represented the new equality under the law. It thus stood for three major ideals of the Enlightenment and the Revolution: technology, humanitarianism, and egalitarianism.

Although the death-dealing apparatus was first proposed in the National Assembly in 1789 by Joseph Guillotin, a public-spirited professor of medicine at the University of Paris, his role in the actual development of the machine was limited. The expert with whom the government consulted two years later to design the instrument was another doctor named Louis, secretary of the Academy of Surgery, who used his knowledge of anatomy and how a blade slices through flesh to design a machine that would cut smoothly through the human neck. The apparatus was constructed by a German harpsichord-maker named Schmidt. It was used for the first time in April 1792 to execute a highwayman who was kept waiting while various improvements and adjustments were made on the machine to ensure its effectiveness. At first the machine was called the Louison or Louisette because of the leading role of Louis in designing it, however when Guillotin first proposed a human decapitating device he had called it *"ma machine."* When a royalist newspaper, *Actes des Apôtres*, published a song, mockingly praising the patriotic doctor for his bright idea and christening the device *"la Guillotine"* to rhyme with *"la machine,"* the name stuck.

The new machine became the principal means of responding to counter-revolutionary activities at the peak of the Revolution. In Paris the guillotine stood in public view not far from the statue of Liberty in the huge square once named after Louis XV, then renamed Place de la Révolution, and later Place de la Concorde. In provincial centres too the guillotine often stood on a conspicuous site because executions were theatrical events intended to impress a lesson on the minds of the citizenry. The machine quickly became a part of French popular culture. It became a theme of popular songs and vaudevilles, and was reproduced in miniature as an ornament in living rooms and as a motif in snuffboxes and china. It was even used on pendants and earrings. For instance, each earring in a pair now preserved in the Carnavalet Museum in Paris consists of a tiny guillotine with the head of a king suspended upside-down underneath it, as though the head is about to drop into a basket.

Above all the guillotine became a symbol for both supporters and opponents of the Revolution. For ardent Revolutionaries it was "the people's avenger," "the national axe," the "republican sword," or "the patriotic shortener." Some even viewed it as a sort of religious object: the Holy Guillotine used in the liturgy of the Red Mass to purify the world. On the other hand, for counterrevolutionaries it was used to represent the excesses of the Revolution. In France during the Terror it would have been fatal to be caught condemning the excessive use of the guillotine, but English caricaturists were free to do so in order to provoke revulsion for the Revolution. In a satirical engraving entitled *A Republican Beau* published in March 1794 when the guillotine was very active, Isaac Cruikshank placed the machine to the right of the *sans-culotte*.[6] In a caricature published in October 1796 depicting the horrors of a successful French invasion of England, *Promis'd Horrors of the French Invasion* (cat. no. 17), Gillray showed a guillotine mounted on the balcony of a London street. And two years later in a series portraying the dire consequences of a French invasion, the same artist depicted a guillotine erected by republican soldiers in place of the throne in the House of Lords to provide a lesson on the Rights of Man to English aristocrats.[7]

After the overthrow of the Robespierrists in July 1794 and the subsequent Thermidorian Reaction (which gets its name from the month in the republican calendar that straddles July/August), French caricaturists were free to satirize overuse of the guillotine during the Terror. One caricature shows Robespierre, among a forest of guillotines, about to decapitate the executioner after the executioner has executed the rest of France.[8] In another complex engraving reminding the public of the horrors of the Terror as a warning for the future, *la Mort*, or Lady Death, wears a tiny guillotine about her neck.[9] Across the Channel the guillotine was too useful a motif to be dropped, even when it was used less frequently in France. Several months after the death of the distinguished French general, Gillray produced *The Apotheosis of General Hoche* in which the commander is shown soaring upward from devastation below, dropping his cavalry boots as he goes.[10] He strums on the rope of a guillotine instead of a lyre and a noose over his head substitutes for a halo. In the midst of the *sans-culotte* heaven, a triangular symbol of Equality replaces that of the Trinity with an inverted decalogue underneath: "Thou Shalt Murder, Thou Shalt Commit Adultery...." Later Gillray even managed to insert a guillotine onto one of the banners in his parody of Napoleon's coronation procession in *The Grand Coronation Procession* (cat. no. 33).

Another striking example of contrasting views on the same phenomenon is French and English treatment of the *sans-culottes*. The term means "without breeches" and originated as a nickname for the male members of the urban lower classes who wore trousers rather than the breeches and hose worn by the males of the upper classes at the time. The *sans-culottes* did not constitute a working-class in the nineteenth-century sense of the word. Shopkeepers, master craftsmen, day labourers, and apprentices were mixed together, thus bridging small proprietors and those who worked for them.[11] They were held together by their way of life, working side by side and sharing the same kind of living conditions and food. At the peak of the

6 Isaac Cruikshank, *A Republican Beau. A Picture of Paris for 1794*; Bibliothèque Nationale, Estampes (hereafter Bib. Nat., Est.), Collection de Vinck (hereafter Coll. de Vinck) 6113; British Museum (hereafter BM) 8435.

7 James Gillray, *We explain the Rights of Man to the Noblesse*, March 1, 1798. No. 1 in the series *Consequences of a Successful French Invasion*; BM 9181.

8 Anonymous, *Robespierre, guillotinant le boureau après avoir fait guillot*ᵗ *tous les Français*; Coll. de Vinck 6359.

9 Anonymous, *Le Miroir du Passé sauvegarde de l'avenir*, Bib. Nat., Est., Qb avril 1797. There is a pamphlet explaining this engraving in Bib. Nat., Imprimés, Lb⁴² 2201.

10 James Gillray, *The Apotheosis of General Hoche*, January 1798, National Portrait Gallery, London; BM 9156.

11 The most authoritative study of the *sans-culottes* is Albert Soboul, *Les Sans-Culottes parisiens en l'an II* (Paris: Librairie Clavreuil, 1958), of which there are several abridged versions in English. Also very good is R. B. Rose, *The Making of the Sans-Culottes* (Manchester: Dover, 1983).

Revolution they were also united by their anxiety over the scarcity of the necessities of life and the soaring cost of living. The politically active members of this social group developed an ideology that combined an emphasis on equality with a demand for direct democracy. They distrusted the deputies in the National Assembly and later the Convention, demanding the right to recall them and to approve or disapprove of the legislation that they enacted.

The power-base of the *sans-culottes* lay in the *sections* or wards of the larger urban centres, especially the forty-eight sections of the city of Paris. In each section they controlled a cluster of institutions – the primary assembly of voters, the popular society or club, and a congeries of administrative bodies. Their power reached its peak after the overthrow of the monarchy, especially a year later in the summer of 1793, following the expulsion of the so-called Girondists from the Convention and the triumph of the Mountain, the name given to the radicals who sat on the high benches in the assembly hall. It was pressure from the *sans-culottes* in Paris in September of that year that forced the Committee of Public Safety to recommend to the Convention the measures that were the basis of the Terror – more ruthless prosecution of suspected counterrevolutionaries, controls over prices, and more vigorous pursuit of the war against enemy states. The power of the *sans-culottes* did not endure for long. The powerful revolutionary government headed by the Committee of Public Safety could not tolerate forty-eight little rival republics in Paris: in the winter and spring of 1793-94 it purged many of their leaders, brought their institutions under central control, and closed their clubs.

At the peak of the Revolution, however, the term *sans-culottes* became a synonym for a zealous Revolutionary, good neighbour, and ideal father. A good description of him is provided by Maréchal's prophetic play, *Le Jugement dernier des rois* (The last judgment of kings), which opened in a Parisian theatre on October 18, 1793, just two days after the execution of Marie-Antoinette.[12] A group of *sans-culottes* arrive to deposit all the former rulers of Europe, including the Pope and Catherine the Great, on a remote volcanic island. To their surprise, they find an old Frenchman who had been exiled to the island twenty years earlier for protesting too vigorously the abduction of his daughter by the king. The newly arrived Frenchmen bring the old man up to date on what has happened back home, using the term *sans-culotte*. When the old man asks what this odd expression means, a *sans-culotte* replies:

> That's for me to tell you. A sans-culotte is a free man. A patriot above all. The
> mass of real people, always good, always wholesome, is made of sans-culottes.
> They are all unblemished citizens, all close to poverty, who eat bread earned by
> the sweat of their brow, who love work, who are good sons, good fathers, good

12 P. Sylvain Maréchal, *Le Jugement dernier des rois, prophétie en un acte...*, Paris: De l'Imp. de C.-F. Patris, imprimeur, l'an second de la République Française).

husbands, good kinsfolk, good friends and good neighbours, but as jealous of their rights as of their duties. Until now, for failing to act in unison, they have been no more than blind and passive tools in the hands of wicked men, that is kings, nobles, priests, self-seekers, aristocrats, statesmen. . . . The sans-culottes, responsible for providing all the needs of the hive, no longer want to tolerate such sluggish and injurious hornets, proud and parasitic, either above us or among us.

OLD MAN: My brothers, my children, I too am a sans-culotte!

One French artist depicted the good *sans-culotte* at home, wearing his tricolour cockade, with his pike nearby ready for action.[13] The same artist portrayed the *sans-culotte*'s wife by the hearth, knitting a red Liberty Bonnet, while a cat plays with the ball of wool.[14] In contrast, English caricaturists depicted the *sans-culotte* as a sort of subhuman, a degenerate fellow who violates the canons of civilized life.[15] Pretending that the term meant that the *sans-culotte* was literally nude from the waist down, English artists showed him in shirt tails, a technique borrowed from vaudeville for making a man look ridiculous. This also provided an opportunity to expose his hairy, misshapen, knock-kneed legs. Another possibility was to exploit the exposed posterior of the man, as in the anonymous engraving *The great Inexpressibles capitulating with a Sans Culotte*, showing the king of Prussia kissing the backside of a *sans-culotte* after the French victory at Valmy, a pictorial version of a vulgar oral expression.[16] At the same time English caricaturists usually depicted the *sans-culotte* with an elongated, enlarged jaw and sunken eyes, making him more ape-like than human.

In addition to portraying the *sans-culotte* as a half-nude, physically regressive specimen of humanity, English caricaturists depicted him and his family violating the most ingrained taboos of modern man. Following the September massacres in 1792, the slaughter of hundreds of suspected counterrevolutionaries held in Parisian prisons, Gillray depicted a *sans-culotte* family devouring a cadaver, breaking the ban on cannibalism among civilized people in *Un petit Souper, a la Parisienne; – or – A Family of Sans-Culotts refreshing, after the fatigues of the day* (fig. 3). In the centre a man, wearing a Liberty Bonnet decorated with a tricoloured cockade, is shown putting into his mouth an eye which he has just gouged out of a severed head. To the left children are shown squatting like animals on the floor while they devour human entrails. In order to exploit the viewer's revulsion for violation of the weak and the beautiful, a female member of the group bastes a child who is roasting on a spit in the background, evoking memory of the Massacres of the Innocents depicted so often in western art. Another *sans-culotte* is seen with his bare buttocks resting on the breasts of a pretty young woman. Moreover, to exploit the male fear of

[13] Anonymous, *Le bon sans Culotte*; Coll. de Vinck 6111.

[14] Anonymous, *Madame sans Culotte*; Coll. de Vinck 6112.

[15] Michel Jouve, "L'image du sans-culotte dans la caricature politique anglaise: naissance d'un stéréotype pictural" in *Gazette des Beaux-Arts*, novembre 1978, 187-196.

[16] Anonymous, *The great Inexpressibles capitulating with a Sans Culotte*, British Museum.

Un petit Souper, a la Parisienne: — or — A Family of Sans Culotts refreshing, after the fatigues of the day.

fig. 3

James Gillray, *Un petit Souper a la Parisienne — or — A Family of Sans-Culotts refreshing, after the fatigues of the day,* September 20, 1792; BM 8122, Coll. de Vinck 6117, engraving, 23.5 x 34.3 cm. By permission of the Bibliothèque Nationale, Paris.

castration, a woman can be seen on the right consuming a pair of testicles. It is a scene of absolute perversion.

English caricaturists also portrayed alleged *sans-culotte* depravity on the street and in the army. In the engraving *A Republican Beau,* Isaac Cruikshank pictured a *sans-culotte* with a fierce expression, wearing a tattered tricoloured suit, fastened on his chest with a dagger.[17] From a side pocket protrudes the body of a child labelled "for a stew." He is armed with spiked club, two pistols, and a bloody dagger. His female counterpart, *A Republican Belle,* also with a violent expression, uses daggers to keep her unruly hair partly under control.[18] She holds a dagger in one hand and a pistol in the other. Without paying attention, she allows a pistol to discharge towards her child who has his arms raised up towards her. Her angular lines, her weapons, and her lack of concern for her child all make her the opposite of the traditional image of the woman as loved-one and mother. In both engravings bodies hang from gallows or lamp-posts in the background. Another English engraver, Robert Newton, in *A Party of the Sans Culotte Army Marching to the Frontier* depicted *sans-culottes* marching into battle, their flags decorated with severed heads, and their Liberty Bonnets enlarged to make them look like fools' caps.[19] In English satirical prints the *sans-culotte* and his wife became types, allegorical figures representing the dark depths of human nature which the Revolution purportedly had opened up.

The different ways artists in the two countries treated weapons is revealing. Revolution involves the use of force or the threat of force to attempt an abrupt change in the existing order; consequently French

[17] See note 6.

[18] Isaac Cruikshank, *A Republican Belle. A Picture of Paris for 1794;* Coll. de Vinck 6114; BM 8436.

[19] Robert Newton, *A Party of the Sans Culotte Army Marching to the Frontier;* BM 8123.

Revolutionaries often treated weapons as quasi-religious objects. The goddess Liberty usually carried a pike, the weapon of the common people. Often the fasces, the symbol of state power and the unity of the Republic, was composed of pikes rather than the rods used in Roman times. French artists also used the pike as a decoration on membership cards, letterheads, wallpaper, and furniture. The club was another weapon of ordinary citizens which appeared on engravings of the Rights of Man and the new republican calendar. Other symbols of power such as cannon, sabres, and warships proliferated. For English caricaturists these weapons were not semi-sacred objects, but signs of anarchy, of a state of disorder, of people out of control. They depicted such weapons, not held or displayed proudly, but stuck carelessly in a belt or used recklessly. In Gillray's depiction of republican soldiers in control of the House of Commons, the inscription over the Speaker's Chair sums up the message of many caricatures: Confusion to All Order.[20]

The English and French had quite different views of two symbols that the Revolutionaries viewed with reverence: the Liberty Bonnet and the Liberty Tree. The Liberty Bonnet can be traced back to ancient Rome where a cap was given to slaves when they were freed. The French Revolutionary version was generally knit of wool and had a high point that fell over to one side. It was dyed red and usually embellished with a tricolour cockade or rosette. It was worn proudly as a symbol of freedom or used as a decorative motif on the Declarations of the Rights of Man, republican calendars, membership cards, letterheads, and book bindings. English artists attempted to degrade this revolutionary symbol, showing it capping bloody weapons, decorating guillotines, or worn by degenerate men. The Liberty Tree, a symbol that often formed a focal point in revolutionary festivals and also served as a decorative motif, was treated by English artists in the same way. In his *Promis'd Horrors of the French Invasion*, Gillray showed a Liberty Tree capped by a Liberty Bonnet, hastily erected on St. James's Street in London. The print shows Prime Minister Pitt, stripped to the waist and tied to the tree, being thrashed by Fox, the leader of the Opposition, thus turning the symbol of liberty into one of oppression (cat. no. 17).

English and French artists also presented contrasting views of the economic conditions in their two countries. The Revolutionaries claimed that the Revolution would ultimately bring prosperity to all French people. This promise was often symbolized by the figure of Nature, a woman with either huge breasts or two rows of them to signify her bountifulness. In one engraving she is shown breast-feeding a white child on one side and a black one on the other side.[21] *La Nature* was usually accompanied by a cornucopia of fruits, grain, and vegetables around her. In reality, however,

[20] See note 7.

[21] Anonymous, *La Nature*; Bib. Nat., Est., Qb 10 novembre 1793.

Promis'd Horrors of the French INVASION, _or_ _ Forcible Reasons for negociating a Regicide PEACE. Vide _ The Authority of Edmund Burke.

17 James Gillray, *Promis'd Horrors of the French Invasion,* October 20, 1796

the Revolution brought hardship instead of plenty to the lower classes. Even in good years French agriculture could barely feed the population of 26,000,000. When harvests were poor, or insurrection and war disrupted agricultural production and distribution, the problem of supplying the large cities was exacerbated. On top of this there was serious inflation, fueled by the flood of paper money which the government issued in an attempt to solve its financial problems. Meanwhile England, free of revolutionary disturbances and warfare on her own soil, enjoyed relative prosperity.

The difference between what the Revolution promised and the actual economic conditions in France offered a theme that was too good for English caricaturists to miss. In an engraving ironically entitled *French Happiness – English Misery* (fig. 4), Isaac Cruikshank showed on the left four famished Frenchmen in tattered clothes. Nearby a cat is dying of hunger beside a mouse which it is too weak to catch. A bird dies in its cage.

fig. 4

Isaac Cruikshank, *French Happiness – English Misery*, January 3, 1793; BM 8228, Coll. de Vinck 6118, engraving, 21.9 x 38.1 cm. By permission of the Bibliothèque Nationale, Paris.

fig. 5

Jacques-Louis David, *Gouvernement Anglois — l'Anglois né Libre*, May 1794; BM 8463, Coll. de Vinck 4389, engraving, 24.8 x 39.0 cm. By permission of the Bibliothèque Nationale, Paris.

22 James A. Leith, *Media and Revolution: Moulding a New Citizenry during the Terror* (Toronto: Canadian Broadcasting Corporation, 1968).

23 Claudette Hould, "La Propagande d'état par l'estampe durant la Terreur," *Les Images de la Révolution Française* (Paris, 1988), 29-37. This article includes a table of caricatures commissioned by the Committee of Public Safety in Year II of the Republic (September 1793 – September 1794).

On the ground is a Liberty Tree that has been gnawed by mice. On the wall of the house are *assignats*, the paper money that the government poured out, and figures showing war casualties, those of France nearly eighty times those of the coalition ranged against her. Also a crucifix now serves to hang a piece of rope and a dagger. Through the window one glimpses a head on the end of a pike. On the other half of the engraving four healthy English farmers devour hams and pies and drink copious jugs of beer. On the chimney is a bible and a bird sings in its cage nearby. In the background trees are laden with fruit and labourers sow and till the fields.

The Committee of Public Safety, the central organ of the Revolutionary government, tried to counter such negative views of France with propaganda of its own. During the Terror the government launched what Barère called "a vast plan for regeneration," which involved using all the available media – festivals, songs, plays, newspapers, paintings, monuments, and caricatures.[22] The greatest French artist of the period, Jacques-Louis David, was commissioned to turn out caricatures.[23] One of the prints that resulted was entitled sarcastically *Gouvernement Anglois – l'Anglois né Libre* (fig. 5) (English government – the Englishman born free). The English government is represented by the figure of a devil, his skin flayed. This forbidding creature decked with royal decorations is shown seizing upon Commerce. The posterior of the giant forms the head of George III who vomits out a multitude of taxes on his people, throwing some of them to the ground while others flee. The attempt of the French government to create an unfavourable image of conditions in Britain continued into the Napoleonic era. In 1807 an anonymous engraving entitled *le Passé, le Présent, l'Avenir* (fig. 6) (The past, the present, the future) depicted the decline of Britain.

The French and English differed also in their views of republican martyrs and their assassins, in particular the images of Jean-Paul Marat and Charlotte Corday. Marat was a deputy of the Convention and the bloodthirsty publisher of the newspaper *L'Ami du Peuple*. As self-proclaimed Friend of the People, he denounced many of his fellow deputies, called for a temporary dictatorship, and advocated lopping off thousands more heads in order to ensure survival of the Republic. Because he suffered from a disease that caused skin eruptions, he used to work on his newspaper while soaking in a bathtub with wet cloths around his head. This was where Charlotte Corday found him and stabbed him in the chest on July 13, 1793, the eve of the fourth anniversary of the storming of the Bastille. Jacques-Louis David portrayed Marat dying, slumped in his tub, the bloody knife on the floor nearby, and the note from Corday still in his hand. The painting was a revolutionary *pietà*. Robespierre and his colleagues on the Committee of Public Safety were reluctant, however, to idolize such a bloodthirsty

fig. 6

Anonymous, *le Passé. le Present, l'Avenir*, November 1807; Qb¹; BM 10146 (1803), engraving (each design), 17.4 x 11.7 cm. By permission of the Bibliothèque Nationale, Paris.

individual, but the *sans-culottes*, who felt he had indeed been their friend, considered him akin to Christ. Some of them even spoke of the "sacred heart of Marat."

Marat became one of a vertitable cult of martyrs, along with two other heroes, the deputy Lepeletier, who had been assassinated for having voted for the execution of the king, and the radical Chalier, who had been ousted from power and sentenced to death in Lyon. It is significant that there were three major martyrs: they constituted a sort of republican trinity. Their busts were paraded together through the streets in Revolutionary festivals. They also appeared as a group on engravings, little plaques, and jewellery. Marat, however, was the most conspicuous. He was considered a modern Brutus who had helped kill the tyrannical king. In addition he was seen by some radical Revolutionaries as the true father of the people, replacing the false father-figure, Louis XVI. For counterrevolutionaries it was Charlotte Corday who was a female Brutus, striking down a blood-thirsty would-be despot. "I killed one man to save thousands," she stated defiantly at her trial before mounting the guillotine. In England she was the hero. In the engraving *The heroic Charlotte la Cordé* (cat. no. 14) Gillray showed her defiance in front of the Revolutionary Tribunal where the judges and the clerks have animal-like features. Isaac Cruikshank showed her striking down Marat, and called her "a second Jean d'Arc." [24]

Of course the French and English presented very different images of the battles in which they were involved. For example, the Revolutionaries were jubilant over the recapture of the important naval base of Toulon on the Mediterranean coast, which had been turned over to the English in August 1793 by moderates opposed to arbitrary Jacobin rule in the city and extremism in Paris. In return for English aid the moderates swore allegiance to Louis XVII, the son of the guillotined king. A three-month siege by the republican army followed. Napoleon Bonaparte, then twenty-four

fig. 7

Anonymous, *Départ de l'Anglais du Continent*, c.1794; Coll. de Vinck 4693, coloured engraving and etching, 28.6 x 19.7 cm. By permission of the Bibliothèque Nationale, Paris.

24 [Isaac Cruikshank], *A Second Jean d'Arc or the Assassination of Marat by Charlotte Cordé of Caen in Normandy on Sunday July 14, 1793 . . .*, Bib. Nat., Est., vol. 32, no. 5298. Although unsigned it seems to be by Cruikshank.

The heroic Charlotte la Cordé, *upon her Trial, at the bar of the Revolutionary Tribunal of Paris, July 17.ᵗʰ 1793, for having rid the world of that monster of Atheism and Murder, the Regicide MARAT, whom she Stabbed in a bath, where he had retired on account of a Leprosy, with which, Heaven had begun the punishment of his Crimes.*
"The noble enthusiasm with which this Woman met the charge, & the elevated disdain, with which she treated the self created Tribunal, struck the whole assembly with terror & astonishment."

Wretches,
— I did not expect to appear before you.
I always thought that I should be delivered up to the rage of the people, torn in pieces, & that my head stuck on the top of of a pike, would have preceded Marat on his state bed, to serve as a rallying point to Frenchman, if there still are any worthy of that name. —But happen what will, if I have the honours of the guillotine, & my clay cold remains are buried, they will soon have conferred upon them the honours of the Pantheon; and my memory will be more honoured in France than that of Judith in Bethulia."

14 James Gillray, *The heroic Charlotte la Cordé*, July 29, 1793

years old, commanded the artillery of the republican forces and helped to plan a decisive attack on the city in December. A reign of terror followed the entry of republican troops into the city, taking more than a thousand victims, but for the Revolutionaries it was a cause for great celebration. Festivals, plays, songs, and engravings were produced to commemorate the victory. One engraving entitled *Départ de l'Anglais du Continent* (fig. 7) (The departure of the Englishman from the continent) shows a sad Englishman, very likely meant to be the Duke of York, abandoning a fort with a breach in its wall. On his back he carries a windmill with a miller inside, an allusion to the English promise to supply grain to the opponents of the central government. In a field nearby a boxer, perhaps representing

FRENCH-TELEGRAPH making SIGNALS in the Dark.

Pitt, measures himself against an ass, which lashes out at another English-man behind it.

When the English won an important victory it was their turn to gloat. At the end of 1797 France was at peace with all the major European powers with the exception of England. The Directory, as the French government was then called, searched for a policy that would force England to make peace before London could create a new coalition. The Directors were faced with two alternatives. The first was to launch an invasion across the Channel to bring England to her knees. The second was to launch an attack on English colonies, which would reduce England's trade and make it financially impossible to continue the war. When the first alternative failed because the French could not muster enough ships for the cross-channel attack, they decided in 1798 to order Bonaparte to launch an attack on Egypt and use it as an advanced base for an attack on Great Britain's holdings in India. After occupying Egypt, Napoleon was to send troops via the Red Sea to French islands in the Indian Ocean, poised to attack India.

The French strategy depended on the ability to keep open a supply line

15 James Gillray, *French-Telegraph making Signals in the Dark*, January 26, 1795

22

Sauve qui peut
ou
LES ANGLAIS EMBARQUANT LEURS VILLES.

à Paris chez Martinet Libraire, Rue du Coq St Honoré

32 Anonymous (French), *Sauve qui peut, ou Les Anglais embarquant leur villes,* 1803

25 James Gillray, *Extirpation of the Plagues of Egypt; Destruction of Revolutionary Crocodiles – or – the British Hero Cleansing yᵉ Mouth of yᵉ Nile,* National Portrait Gallery, London, and the Bib. Nat., Est., vol. 53, no. 7389; BM 9250.

between France and the expeditionary force. The first phase of the operation went well. Bonaparte's force sailed from Toulon in May 1798, captured the island of Malta, anchored its fleet in Aboukir Bay, and then occupied much of Egypt. Meanwhile the British had sent Admiral Nelson to hunt down the French fleet. Eventually he found it in August lying at anchor. In the ensuing battle the British scored a decisive victory, destroying most of the French fleet. The French Army of the East was left isolated and once again foreign powers were encouraged to join in the struggle against France. The victory thus changed the whole strategic situation: at the end of 1797 France was at peace with the Continent and England was isolated; in 1799 France was isolated and England was leading another coalition against her. The French army was able to hang on in Egypt, but Napoleon left his army and returned home. Naturally English caricaturists celebrated this event. For example, Gillray made an engraving entitled *Extirpation of the Plagues of Egypt* showing Nelson in the water almost up to his knees, using a club of "British Oak" to exterminate tricoloured crocodiles (the French fleet) at the mouth of the Nile.[25]

It was in the depiction of Napoleon, whose meteoric rise began with the French recapture of Toulon, that we find the most extreme depictions of the same phenomenon. Napoleon was the most caricatured personality of the day. Only in the twentieth century when cartoons have appeared in mass-circulation newspapers has he been bypassed by caricaturists for such leaders as Roosevelt, Churchill, Hitler, and de Gaulle. The Corsican began to get attention from French engravers after he used the famous "whiff of grapeshot" to put down a Parisian insurrection on 13 Vendémiaire Year IV of the republican calendar, or October 5, 1795. The following spring he was made commander-in-chief of the French army in Italy. Before setting out he married Josephine Beauharnais and altered his name from Buonaparte to the more French Bonaparte. In Italy the troops under his command won a succession of victories over Austro-Sardinian forces, triumphs commemorated by French engravers. After these victories engraved portraits of him began to appear in London in the summer of 1796. His successes in Italy raised fears of a French invasion of England, a threat that inspired Gillray's *Promis'd Horrors of the French Invasion* (cat. no. 17).[26]

Napoleon aroused the attention of English engravers again as commander of a projected invasion of England in 1798, and then, in the same year, as commander of the French expedition to Egypt that was left stranded after Nelson's brilliant victory at the mouth of the Nile. Then there was a brief interlude until Napoleon seized power in France by the coup of 18-19 Brumaire, November 9 and 10, 1799. The Directory, established by a conservative republican constitution in August 1795, had proved extremely unstable. The regime had to steer a path between a return of the monarchy on the one side, and a return of the radical Jacobinism of the Terror on the other. Financial difficulties and unending warfare made survival of the regime even more difficult. Napoleon's coup, which terminated the Directory, was the fourth coup in three years. In a caricature entitled *Exit Libertè à la Francois! – or – Buonaparte closing the Farce of Egalitè at Sᵗ Cloud. . .* (the artist never mastered French accents), Gillray showed the general directing his soldiers to dismiss the legislators of the Directory.[27] The wounds on Napoleon's face and hands are evidence of a myth that there had been an attempt on his life, a story that helped arouse sympathy for him.

English caricaturists delighted in emphasizing the instability of the French government. There was a factual basis for their satire: the first constitution drafted by the Revolutionaries, which had been completed in September 1791, had lasted only until the overthrow of the monarchy less than a year later; the second constitution, completed by the Montagnard Convention in June 1793 and accepted by the voters, had never been put

41 Anonymous (British), *Napoleon . . . Make Peace With!!!*, March/April 1814

26 See also pages 18 and 56.

27 James Gillray, *Exit Libertè a la Francois! – or – Buonaparte closing the Farce of Egalitè at Sᵗ Cloud Novʳ 10th, 1799*, Bib. Nat., Est., vol. 54, no. 7416; BM 9250 and 9250A.

Publ.d by R. Ackermann, 101 Strand London

NAPOLEON

THE FIRST, and LAST, by the Wrath of Heaven Emperor of the Jacobins, Protector of the Confederation of Rogues, Mediator of the Hellish League, Grand Cross of the Legion of Horror, Commander in Chief of the Legions of Skeletons left at Moscow, Smolensk, Leipzig, &c. Head Runner of Runaways, Mock High-Priest of the Sanhedrim, Mock Prophet of Mussulmen, Mock Pillar of the Christian Faith, Inventor of the Syrian Method of disposing of his own Sick by sleeping Draughts, or of captured Enemies by the Bayonet; First Grave-Digger for burying alive; Chief Gaoler of the Holy Father and of the King of Spain, Destroyer of Crowns, and Manufacturer of Counts, Dukes, Princes, and Kings; Chief Douanier of the Continental System, Head Butcher of the Parisian and Toulonese Massacres, Murderer of Hoffer, Palm, Wright, nay, of his own Prince, the noble and virtuous Duke of Enghien, and of a thousand others; Kidnapper of Ambassadors, High-Admiral of the Invasion Praams, Cup-Bearer of the Jaffa Poison, Arch-Chancellor of Waste-Paper Treaties, Arch-Treasurer of the Plunder of the World, the sanguinary Coxcomb, Assassin, and Incendiary......to

MAKE PEACE WITH!!!

This Hieroglyphic Portrait of the DESTROYER is faithfully copied from a German Print, with the Parody of his assumed Titles. The *Hat* of the Destroyer represents a discomfited French Eagle, maimed and crouching, after his Conflict with the Eagles of the North. His *Visage* is composed of the Carcases of the Victims of his Folly and Ambition, who perished on the Plains of Russia and Saxony. His Throat is encircled with the *Red Sea*, in Allusion to his drowned Hosts. His Epaulette is a *Hand*, leading the Rhenish Confederation, under the flimsy Symbol of a *Cobweb*. The *Spider* is an Emblem of the Vigilance of the Allies, who have inflicted on that Hand a deadly Sting!

PUBLISHED AT R. ACKERMANN'S, 101, STRAND, LONDON.

Harrison & Leigh, Printers, 373, Strand.

The above are true Likeness(es) of CAMBACERES, — LE BRUN, — the ABBE SEYES, and BUONAPARTE, drawn at Paris Nov.r 1799

The French-Consular-Triumverate, settling the New Constitution,

with a Peep at the Constitutional Pigeon Holes of the Abbe Seyes in the Back Ground.

21 James Gillray, *The French-Consular-Triumverate*,
    January 1, 1800

into effect because of counterrevolution and war; the third constitution, passed in September 1795, followed the overthrow of Robespierre and the subsequent Thermidorian reaction, and lasted just over four years. Gillray satirized this succession of constitutions in his engraving entitled *The French-Consular-Triumverate* (cat. no. 21). The print emphasizes the domination of Napoleon, the First Consul, who is writing while the other two consuls, Cambacérès and Lebrun, hold the tips of their plumes between their lips. The Abbé Sieyès, who had proposed a plan of his own, looks through a window at bundles of old constitutions in storage, with a guillotine at the top. On the table is a constitution for the future, predicting that Bonaparte will become "Grand Monarque."

Napoleon was most admired in England during the temporary lull in the warfare between England and France that followed the Treaty of Amiens, signed in March 1802. Britain gave up most of its conquests made during the Revolutionary wars, and France agreed to withdraw from Naples. Gillray satirized the halt in hostilities in a print entitled *The First Kiss this Ten Years! – or – the Meeting of Britannia and Citizen Francois*, which Napoleon is said to have found very amusing.[28] A tall French soldier, who has let his sword fall to the floor, leans over to kiss a short, plump Britannia, who has put aside her trident and shield:

FRANCOIS: Madame, permittez me to pay my profound esteem to your engaging person! and to seal on your divine Lips my everlasting attachment!!

BRITANNIA: Monsieur, you are really a well bred Gentleman! And tho' you make me blush, yet you kiss so delicately that I cannot refuse you, tho' I was sure you would deceive me again!!

On the wall overhead, Napoleon and George III stare unsmilingly at each other from within oval frames.

When the peace broke down as Britannia had anticipated, Napoleon became the chief villain in English caricatures. As his control over the continent grew, English caricaturists, especially Gillray, diminished his stature. Although earlier Gillray had shown Napoleon as an impressive figure, he now reduced him to a pygmy. "Little Boney" became familiar in English prints. In June 1803 Gillray lampooned him in an engraving entitled *The King of Brobdingnag, and Gulliver*.[29] George III examines a tiny figure of Bonaparte, exclaiming:

My little friend Gildrig, you have made a most admirable panegyric of yourself and Country, but from what I can gather from your own relation and the answers I have with much pains wringed and extorted from you, that I cannot but conclude you to be one of the most pernicious, little odious reptiles that nature ever suffered to crawl upon the face of the earth.

28 James Gillray, *The First Kiss this ten Years! – or –
    the meeting of Britannia and Citizen Francois*;
    Coll. de Vinck 7581; BM 9960 and 9960A.

29 James Gillray, *The King of Brobdingnag, and
    Gulliver*, June 26, 1803; BM 10019.

SNUFFING OUT BONEY!

43 George Cruikshank, *Snuffing Out Boney!,* May 1, 1814

As Napoleon set up satellite states, mostly ruled by his relatives, Gillray ridiculed him as a baker turning out a batch of gingerbread kings. English caricaturists naturally gloated over the beginnings of disintegration of the great Empire, commencing in Spain. One caricature following an insurrection in Madrid showed the Emperor trying vainly to fend off a horde of locusts.[30] Later when Napoleon had to retreat from Russia, beaten by the weather as well as by Russian resistance, William Elmes engraved *General Frost Shaving Little Boney*, showing a giant figure blasting out frigid wind from his nostrils and using Russian steel to shave the Emperor.[31] General

30 [Williams], *Spanish Flies or Boney taking an immoderate Dose*; Bib. Nat., Est., Tf 457, vol. 1; BM 11016.

31 [William Elmes], *General Frost Shaving Little Boney*, Bib. Nat., Est., Tf 457, vol. 1; BM 11917.

53 Attributed to Thomas Rowlandson, *Vive Le Roi! Vive L'Empereur. Vive Le Diable*, April/May 1815

VIVE LE ROI! __ VIVE L'EMPEREUR.
VIVE LE DIABLE

Frost tramples tiny figures of French soldiers under his massive paw-like feet. George Cruikshank showed in *Snuffing Out Boney!* (cat. no. 43) a terrifying Cossack using a candle extinguisher to snuff out Boney, a scene repeated in a picture on the wall. In 1814 Thomas Rowlandson showed the Prussian commander, General Blücher, holding up a fox with the head of Bonaparte, about to be thrown to hounds representing Wellington, the Duke of York, the Austrian Schwarzenberg, and the Russian Kutuzov.[32]

In 1815, with the final defeat of Napoleon and the return of Louis XVIII to the French throne, English caricatures once again depicted the instability of France. Rowlandson ridiculed the ease with which the French welcomed Napoleon one month and the Bourbon king the next in *Vive le Roi! Vive L'Empereur. Vive Le Diable* (cat. no. 53). In this print a French

32 Thomas Rowlandson, *Coming in at the Death of the Corisican Fox*, Bib. Nat., Est., Tf 457, vol. 3; BM 11220.

THE FOX & THE GOOSE; OR, BONEY BROKE LOOSE!

Published March 17, 1815, by WHITTLE & LAURIE, 53, Fleet Street, London.

soldier wears a hat that declares three allegiances: to the Emperor, to the King, and to the Devil. The windmill in the background sarcastically symbolizes French stability in which regimes change with the wind. The defeat of Napoleon left the two countries with different memories. England commemorated the outcome with the Nelson Monument, Trafalgar Square, and Waterloo Station. France preferred to remember the happier events with the Arc de Triomphe, the Avenue de la Grande Armée, the Vendôme column crowned with a statue of Napoleon, and streets, squares, and bridges named after French triumphs. A tour of Paris evokes the Empire at its peak.

The restoration of the Bourbons saw caricatures turn largely to social satire, but the two countries often still viewed each other differently. Peace brought a long-postponed chance for the English to visit Paris, see the *Salons* in the Louvre where the art of the day was exhibited, try French cuisine, gawk at the extravagant Parisian fashions, try the new rides available in amusement parks, or skate on the Canal de l'Ourcq when it was

52 George Cruikshank, *The Fox & The Goose; or, Boney Broke Loose!,* March 17, 1815

40 Thomas Rowlandson, *The Devils Darling,* March 12, 1814

Pub. March 12 1814 by R. Ackermann N 101 Strand

THE DEVILS DARLING.

Le Thé Anglais.

50 Anonymous (French), *Le Thé Anglais,* January 1815

LA COURSE DES MONTAGNES RUSSES A PARIS.

Le Suprême Bon-Ton. N.° 29.

à Paris chez Martinet   Déposé &ª

65 Adrien-Pierre-François Godefroy, *La Course des
Montagnes Russes à Paris* from *Le Suprême Bon
Ton, No. 29,* November 1816

Les Anglais au Salon de 1814.

47 Louis-Félix Legendre, *Les Anglais au Salon de 1814*,
November 2, 1814

fig. 8

Anonymous, *L'Anglais et le Français ou Chacun son gout,* October 15, 1816; Coll. de Vinck 7694, coloured engraving and etching, 18.8 x 29.2 cm. By permission of the Bibliothèque Nationale, Paris.

L'ANGLAIS ET LE FRANÇAIS ou CHACUN SON GOUT.

unusually cold. In England George Cruikshank produced a print entitled *Traveling in France – or, – Le depart dela diligence* (cat. no. 71), which gently satirized a coachload of English folk touring France. He included a French veteran in the scene, very likely crippled in the recent wars, a reminder of the struggles of the recent past. In *Les Anglais au Salon de 1814* (cat. no. 47) the French artist Legendre lampooned English tourists viewing the latest paintings, their expressions revealing shock, disgust, and boredom. Another artist in *Le Thé Anglais* (cat. no. 50) made fun of conservatively dressed English women drinking tea with a scrawny English officer. Other artists ridiculed gluttonous Englishmen, as in *L'Anglais et le Français ou Chacun son Gout* (fig. 8), fat John Bull devouring French food while Frenchmen delicately court beautiful women. Such stereotypes of "the other" die hard. "Plus ça change, plus c'est la même chose."

James A. Leith, Department of History, Queen's University

35

COLOUR PLATES

27 Jean-François Bosio, *Bal de l'Opera* from *Cinq Tableaux de costumes Parisiens,* 1804

Garde d'Honneur',
finishing the Procession.

Senator Fouché,
Intendant General of ye Police,
bearing the Sword of Justice.

Bertheir, Bernadotte, Augerou
& all the brave Train of Republican
-Generals, marching in the Procession.

Puissant Continental Powers,
Train-Bearers to the Emperor.

Ladies of Honor.
(cidivant, Poissardes)
Train Bearers to ye Empress.

33 James Gillray, *The Grand Coronation Procession,* January 1, 1805

Buonaparte au Bain.

Le Tyran de la france, dans une baignoire de Cristal fait couler tour à tour le sang et les larmes des français, il se plait a nager au milieu.
L'ange du nord vient consoler la france et lui rend les lis et l'Olivier de la paix.

42 Anonymous, *Buonoparte au Bain*, Spring 1814

Les Anglais au Canal de L'Ourc.

Paris chez Martinet, Rue du Coq, No. 15.

49 Anonymous, *Les Anglais au Canal de L'Ourc*, January 25, 1815

Le désarroi.

à Paris chez Beaublé fils, quai des augustins, N.º 37.

38 Anonymous, *Le désarroi*, September 1814

Monsieur Calicot partant pour le Combat des Montagnes.

66 Anonymous, *Monsieur Calicot partant pour le Combat des Montagnes*, August 1817

71 George Cruikshank, *Traveling in France — or, — Le depart dela diligence,* October 19, 1818

CATALOGUE OF THE EXHIBITION

James A. Leith and Andrea Joyce

THE OLD REGIME

ANONYMOUS
French, late 18th century

1 *La Brillante Toillete de la Déesse du Gout*   c.1770 (see p. 8)
Etching and engraving on laid paper
29.0 x 19.0 cm (imp.)
Gift of the Trier-Fodor Foundation, 1982
Acc. no. 82/257

Although there were a large number of political caricatures circulating in France during the eighteenth century, the numerous print collectors of the time were primarily interested in social satires. They touched on such widely varied subjects as Voltaire, doctors, and aeronautic balloons. Ultimately it was caricatures based on fashion and manners that composed the bulk of the satirical works (Grand-Carteret, 25 - 40; Arséne, 85 - 95).

Social satire, and for that matter all prints in the eighteenth century, can be divided into two groups. The first are the moralistic, sentimental works that won popularity among the poorer classes and the women of the middle class. The second group, "les galantes," are the prints that expressed the frivolity, the "joie de vivre" of the eighteenth century; they are naughty, lustful, indeed scandalous renderings of women with their lovers. These erotic prints, which found their way into the homes of the nobility and upper middle class (Adhémar, 152-154), are symptomatic of the decadence of the aristocracy. The contrast between the two genres is epitomized in the moralistic, didactic paintings of Greuze and the frivolous, licentious works of Fragonard.

La Brillante Toillete de la Déesse du Gout falls into the second category. In this scene a fashionable lady, wearing one of the large headpieces of the period, dresses while her lover whispers in her ear. It was common practice for women to receive gentlemen visitors in the boudoir regardless of the state of undress. Even when in the bath women might receive guests, pouring milk into the bath water to retain some level of modesty (Corson, *Make-up*, 289).   A.J.

ANONYMOUS
French, late 18th century

2 *L'Incendie des Coeffures*   c.1770
Etching and engraving on laid paper
28.8 x 18.8 cm
Gift of the Trier-Fodor Foundation, 1982
Acc. no. 82/259

A major topic of eighteenth-century satirists was the fashion for huge, ornate wigs. While caricatures of these elaborate wigs were

2 Anonymous (French), *L'Incendie des Coeffures,* c.1770

delightfully entertaining, they also provided acerbic comments on the excesses of the Old Regime.

The "pouf," as women's hair styles were called, were huge wigs built on cushions and wire supports, embellished with human, horse, cow, or fox hair. These constructions, which reached heights of two to three feet (Corson, *Hair*, 333) were decorated with flowers, feathers, fruit, vegetables, lace, or ribbons. Sometimes they were designed to commemorate an event: the addition of a ship might celebrate a naval victory. Hog grease, tallow, or pomatum was used to solidify the colossal mass of hair, creating a texture similar to that of papier-mâché (Cunnington, *Costume in Eighteenth Century*, 246-258, 355-377).

Given the complex construction of the wigs and the general lack of concern for sanitation at that time – Marie Antoinette considered simply washing her hands sufficient (Payne, 437) while others prided themselves on never having washed their faces with water (Corson, *Make-up*, 288-289); hair pieces were changed every few weeks at most. Not surprisingly scalp irritation, hair loss, toothache, earache and blotchiness ensued (Mercier, *Waiting City*, 164). Worst of all was the "noisome dirt" – lice (Mercier, *Picture of Paris*, 29). At night, a large cage or bandage was placed over the hair, not as one might expect, to protect the hair, but rather to prevent the wig from infiltration by rats (Mercier, *Waiting City*, 164).

The fashion for wigs was so great that at one point it led to the employment of 1,200 wigmakers and 6,000 assistants in Paris alone (Mercier, *Picture of Paris*, 16). Not everyone condoned this fashion. One eighteenth-century observer wrote disapprovingly of the fact that "the powder with which two hundred thousand individuals whiten their hair is drawn from the food of the poor," and that "the flour which is used on the lawyer's full-bottomed wig...would feed ten thousand unfortunate beings" (Mercier, *Picture of Paris*, 15).   A.J.

ANONYMOUS
French, late 18th century

3 *Le Dîner misterieux*   c.1770
Etching and engraving on laid paper
29.0 x 18.8 cm (imp.)
Gift of the Trier-Fodor Foundation, 1982
Acc. no. 82/258

Le Dîner misterieux continues the satire on the fashion and manners of the eighteenth century. Here, two flirtatious couples dine. One of the gentlemen appears to be a priest.

There were no limits to the vanities of the fashionable in the eighteenth century. Gentlemen wore rouge, tight breeches and stuffed parchment or wool in their stockings to enhance the muscle tone of their calves (Cunnington, *Costume in Eighteenth Century*, 213, 261). It was said of women that fashion ruled their lives "with an unpitying rigor" (Weigert, 1). Adding to the discomforts of cumbersome wigs, women constricted their bodies with tight corsets and stiff-boned bodices. They used large quantities of rouge composed of lead chalk, corrosive to the skin, and applied mouse skin to their foreheads to supplement the plucked eyebrows. Pads of wool and flannel called "bosom friends" were stuffed inside bodices to enhance the bust; and the roundness of a lady's cheeks was augmented with "cork plumpers," pieces of cork placed inside the mouth (Cunnington, *Costume in Eighteenth Century*, 388-389; Corson; *History of Make-up*, 245-256). In fact, fashion even altered the design of furniture: the seats of chairs were widened to accommodate the bulky skirts, and the backs were lowered so that a woman wearing a large wig could sit up straight (Black, 225).   A.J.

LE DÎNER MISTERIEUX

3 Anonymous (French), *Le Dîner misterieux*, c.1770

MATTHEW DARLY
British, 18th century
after HENRY BUNBURY
British, 1750-1811

4 *The Kitchen of a French Post House (La Cuisine de la Poste)*
      February 1, 1771
BM 4764
Engraving on laid paper
41.8 x 44.7 cm (sheet, trimmed at platemark)
Gift of the Trier-Fodor Foundation, 1985
Acc. no. 85/46

Matthew Darly was a professional engraver active in London around 1754 to 1778. He and his wife Mary, also an accomplished artist, were the proprietors of a well-known print shop in London and were great innovators in the marketing and selling of popular prints (Hill, *Satirical Etchings*, xv). In the 1760s and 1770s caricature was considered a fashionable hobby and it was common practice for an amateur to pass a sketch or an idea to a profes-

4　Matthew Darly after Henry Bunbury, *The Kitchen of a French Post House (La Cuisine de la Poste)*, February 1, 1771

sional engraver who would then reproduce it for the amateur to keep or sell in a print shop. Although Darly engraved *The Kitchen of a French Post House*, the inspiration for the work actually came during a trip to France from the sketches made by Henry Bunbury, an amateur engraver (George, *Hogarth to Cruikshank*, 144).

There were many English travellers in France in the eighteenth century: apparently 40,000 English visitors passed through Calais between 1763 and 1765 (George, *Hogarth to Cruikshank*, 144). *The Kitchen of a French Post House* depicts an English visitor's first encounter with the French. The most curious figure is the postilion, the driver of the coach that transported the travellers from Calais to Paris. He wore a dirty night cap and huge boots made of wood and iron (George, *Hogarth to Cruikshank*, 144), and amazed the English passengers by running back and forth between the carriage and horses without stopping the vehicle (Scott, 30). In Darly's work the postilion, wearing the immense boots, comes forward to greet an English traveller.

Darly's work also captures the austere interior of the various post houses and hotels where the coach stopped to change horses and pay tolls. The English were dismayed by these sparsely furnished buildings; they lacked carpets, a parlour, and the furniture was of appalling quality (Maxwell, 30). There were also many complaints about the lack of cleanliness. Rats and insects were everywhere, making it impossible in some cases for visitors to sleep in the bed; and garbage was often thrown out the window into the courtyard (Maxwell, 30).

In this print the French peasants wear wooden shoes called "*sabots*," filled with wool or straw to make them fit (Duffy, 37). In contemporary English satire these shoes symbolized the horrors of despotism. The English believed the French were so overburdened by the taxes of their tyrannical king, that they could not afford to buy comfortable leather shoes (Duffy, 34-35).　A.J.

ROBERT POLLARD
British, 1755-1838, and
FRANCIS JUKES
British, 1747-1812
after THOMAS ROWLANDSON
British, 1756-1827

5　*Vaux-hall Gardens*　June 28, 1785
BM 6853
Grego, I, 156-164
Hand-coloured etching and aquatint on laid paper
48.0 x 73.2 cm (comp.)
Gift of J. T. Johnson, and Marion Darte Johnson, 1982
Acc. no. 82/227

5　Robert Pollard and Francis Jukes after Thomas Rowlandson, *Vauxhall Gardens,* June 28, 1785

In 1785 an exhibition of English caricatures was held in Paris, and in 1790 a London print shop charged an entrance fee of one shilling to view a display of French and English caricatures. By the 1790s satirists on both sides of the Channel were aware of each other's work (Adhémar, 191). At this time prints were published with the intention of being sold in both France and England. The title of Debucourt's *La Promenade de la Gallerie du Palais Royal* (1787) was printed in French and English to facilitate its sale in both countries (Adhémar, 174). No artist in France or elsewhere could rival the leading English satirists at the end of the eighteenth and the beginning of the nineteenth centuries. It was not until the end of the Empire that French and German satirists took the lead. Until that time, English satire dominated on the Continent and greatly influenced the development of satire in France (Brown University 10; Adhémar, 191; Champfleury, 246).

One of the most popular English satirists on the Continent was Thomas Rowlandson (Adhémar, 191). Rowlandson was prolific, producing nearly 10,000 drawings and 2,500 prints (cited in Rix, 2). He specialized in humorous scenes of society, depicting the manners and characters of his time. Rowlandson was in France during the 1770s and 1780s and his style shows the influence of the French rococo (Rix, 4).

Vaux-hall Gardens, a watercolour exhibited at the Royal Academy in 1781 and reproduced in a print in 1785, "rapidly became famous on both sides of the English Channel" (Baltimore, 279). In this work Rowlandson presents a "social panorama" of fashionable figures at one of the pleasure gardens in London. "Everyone went to Vauxhall," it was a place to stroll, dine, dance, and listen to music. Vauxhall was one of the more exclusive gardens, opening in the spring and closing in August when the "quality" left the city (George, *Hogarth to Cruikshank,* 77). Rowlandson frequented the pleasure gardens, as his friend explained, "to study character" (Grego, I, 156).

Vaux-hall Gardens is a lively and amusing portrait of fashionable society in London on the eve of the French Revolution.　A.J.

6 Anonymous (French), *Bon, nous voila d'accord,* June/July 1789

ANONYMOUS
French, 18th century

6 *Bon, nous voila d'accord*   June/July 1789
Coll. de Vinck 2051
Hand-coloured etching on grey laid paper
17.0 x 13.8 cm
On loan from David Bindman

This print from early in the Revolution illustrates the hope that the three Estates – the Clergy, the Nobility, and the Commoners – would work together for the regeneration of France. The anonymous artist shows representatives of the three orders playing their different instruments in harmony. On the left an abbot plays a horn known as a serpent, in the centre a commoner plays a violin, and on the right a noble plays a flute. The phrase *être d'accord* means both to be in tune and to be in agreement.   J. L.

7 Anonymous (French), *Le Voeux accompli,* September/October 1789

ANONYMOUS
French, 18th century

7 *Le Voeux accompli*   September/October 1789
Coll. de Vinck 2058
Hand-coloured etching on blue-grey laid paper
31.8 x 21.4 cm (cut)
On loan from David Bindman

This engraving, too, expressed the hope early in the Revolution that the three orders of the Old Regime would work together. The female figure in the centre represents *la noblesse,* the nobility. She wears a helmet decorated with a plume and holds a sword capped with a red bonnet inscribed with the word "Liberté," the bonnet that became one of the commonest symbols of the Revolution. On her right is a prelate and on her left is a member of the Third

Estate holding a sword in his right hand and leaning on a spade. The serpents on the ground represent various privileges that the Revolution had suppressed.   J.L.

ANONYMOUS
French, 18th century

8   *A Versaille à Versaille*   October 1789
     (see p. 10)
     Coll. de Vinck 2962
     Hand-coloured etching on blue-grey laid paper
     17.8 x 28.0 cm
     On loan from David Bindman

In the seventeenth century Louis XIV had moved the court from Paris to Versailles, about twelve miles from the city where it would be isolated from possible disturbances such as occurred there during his childhood. Versailles remained the seat of government until October 1789 when the royal family was forced to move to Paris.

The events that led to this move are known as the October Days. By the autumn of 1789 the balance of power between Louis XVI and the new National Assembly had not yet been decided. The king was resisting giving his approval to some important legislation. Some aristocrats in the Assembly urged the king to remain firm, while the patriots who formed the majority grew impatient. The patriots, fearing the king might resort to force, looked for support in Paris.

On September 14 Louis sent for the Flanders Regiment. When it arrived in Versailles it was fêted by the king's bodyguard at a banquet during which the revolutionary tricolour was insulted. News of this event intensified the already volatile situation in Paris. The idea developed of organizing a march to Versailles to set things straight. On October 5 several thousand women, excited by economic hardship, gathered at the city hall. The National Guard sympathized with the crowd and the idea of marching to Versailles.

This print shows the departure of the women to Versailles with cannon seized at the city hall and a wide variety of other weapons. On October 6 the king agreed to move with his family to Paris where they became hostages to the Parisians. The Assembly followed soon afterwards to the same hazardous environment. The October Days tilted the balance of power towards the Assembly and exposed the king to popular pressure. The two days also saw women playing a key role at the critical moment in the Revolution.   J.L.

ANONYMOUS
French, 18th century

9   *Triomphe de l'Armée Parisienne réunis au Peuple a son retour de Versailles à Paris le 6 octobre 1789*   October 1789   (see p. 11)
     Coll. de Vinck 2996
     Hand-coloured etching on grey laid paper
     21.6 x 37.1 cm
     On loan from David Bindman

This print shows the Parisian women who had marched to Versailles the previous day returning in triumph along with members of the National Guard who had accompanied them. They carry with them poplar branches (etymologically, "poplar" means "tree of the people"). They also carry the heads of two royal bodyguards butchered when the crowd had invaded the palace.   J.L.

ANONYMOUS
French, 18th century

10   *La famille Des Cochons ramenée dans L'étable*   June/July 1791
      Coll. de Vinck 3787
      Hand-coloured etching on grey laid paper
      15.6 x 22.8 cm
      On loan from David Bindman

This caricature treats the outcome of an event that had profound consequences for the Revolution and the fate of Louis XVI and Marie-Antoinette. The king had become increasingly discontented with his confinement to Paris where he had been a captive since the October Days. He also had become antagonistic to the measures that the National Assembly had passed concerning the church, measures which Pope Pius VI had denounced. On June 21, 1791, the royal family left Paris surreptitiously and headed for the border, hoping to cross it and reach friendly courts. They were recognized at Varennes and forced to return to Paris.

10   Anonymous (French), *La famille Des Cochons ramenée dans L'étable*, June/July 1791

The artist here reduces the royal family to animals who have escaped from the stable, have been rounded up, and are being put back where they belong. A horse ridden by a member of the National Guard pulls a crude cart filled with straw carrying Louis XVI, Marie-Antoinette, Madame Royale, the prince, Monsieur the Count of Provence, and Madame Elizabeth. The print must have been done soon after the arrest of the royal family, before it was known that Monsieur was not among them.

This fiasco for Louis XVI and his family helped to undermine the credibility of the king and the effort to create a constitutional monarchy in France.   J. L.

THOMAS ROWLANDSON
British, 1756-1827

11 *English Barracks*   August 12, 1791 (see entry after cat. no. 12)
    (see p. 2)
    Grego, I, 295
    Hand-coloured etching and aquatint on wove paper
    43.5 x 56.8 cm (sheet)
    Gift of the J. T. Johnson Estate, 1985
    Acc. no. 85/445

THOMAS ROWLANDSON
British, 1756-1827

12 *French Barracks*   August 12, 1791 (see p. 3)
    Grego, I, 295-296
    Hand-coloured etching and aquatint on wove paper
    42.1 x 54.3 cm (imp.)
    Gift of the J. T. Johnson Estate, 1985
    Acc. no. 85/432

This pair of satires by Thomas Rowlandson represents a theme that was prominent in eighteenth-century English caricature, that of comparing the hearty English with the emaciated French. This graphic motif can be traced back to William Hogarth's *Gate of Calais, or O the Roast Beef of Old England* (1749) in which a robust English cleric licks a slab of roast beef (fig. 9) – the juices of which were thought to imbue the English with a sturdy and sound disposition – while the skinny French starve on frogs and thin stews. Hogarth's image captured the English conception that the French of the Old Regime were miserably poor and vain (Duffy, 35).

In these caricatures the scrawny, foppish French soldier with his long queue, powdered wig, and huge boots looks ridiculous by comparison with the sturdy, wholesome English soldier. Published in 1791, the year in which English praise for the Revolution turned into bitter criticism, Rowlandson's works take on propagandistic proportions (Duffy, 280).   A. J.

fig. 9   William Hogarth, *Gate of Calais, or O the Roast Beef of England, &c.*, March 1749; BM 3050, etching and engraving, 34.5 x 44.3 cm. Reproduced by permission of the Trustees of the British Museum.

JAMES GILLRAY
British, 1757-1815

13 *The Zenith of French Glory*   February 12, 1793 (see
    frontispiece)
    BM 8300
    Hand-coloured etching on wove paper
    35.5 x 25.0 cm (imp.)
    Gift of the Trier-Fodor Foundation, 1982
    Acc. no. 82/245

During the first few years of the French Revolution, England was generally enthusiastic and supportive of the French cause. Sympathetic societies were established in England, boots and supplies were sent to the French army (Rudé, 185), and the great English satirist James Gillray executed a pro-Revolutionary satire. However, in the wake of the attempted escape of the royal family and the increasing violence of the Revolutionaries, English enthusiasm waned, and following the execution of the king in 1793, there was only scathing criticism (Duffy, 38).

One of the most poignant of Gillray's satires is *The Zenith of French Glory*. This satire is based on the execution of Louis XVI, which took place on January 21, 1793 in the Place de la Révolution. The guillotine in this etching was the first realistic rendition of the decapitating machine to be seen in England. Hanging from street lanterns are a judge with the scales of justice askew, a bishop, and two monks. On the right, the cap of "Libertas" crowns a bishop's staff, and in the niche the crucified Christ cries out, "Bon Soir Monsieur." A *sans-culotte*, perched on a street lantern, looks gleefully upon the scene. This coarse, lewd figure plays the fiddle while the dome of a church, probably that of the Church of the Assumption, goes up in flames. He wears the symbolic red bonnet of liberty with "Ça Ira," the title of a popular Revolutionary song, emblazoned on it (Hill, *Satirical Etchings*, 105; BM 8300). In this print Gillray bemoans the French Revolution's apparent abandonment of the ideals of 1789. He also reveals British opinion, which held that the death of the king rang the death knell for civilized society in France while it ushered in a new era of anarchy and bloodshed (George, *English Political Caricature 1793-1832*, 2-3).   A.J.

JAMES GILLRAY
British, 1757-1815

14 *The heroic Charlotte la Cordé*   July 29, 1793 (see p. 21)
(see p. 21)
BM 8336
Coll. de Vinck 5352
Etching on wove paper
32.0 x 37.5 cm
Gift of the Trier-Fodor Foundation, 1988
Acc. no. 88/108

Charlotte Corday, a young woman from Caen who sympathized with moderates, assassinated Jean-Paul Marat, the bloodthirsty editor of the paper *L'Ami du Peuple*, as he worked in his bath on July 13, 1793. Marat suffered from a disease that caused painful skin eruptions which were alleviated by soaking in a solution. Corday was seized at the scene, tried before the Revolutionary Tribunal, and sentenced to be guillotined. News of the assassination reached London on July 22 and Gillray's caricature was published on July 29.

Gillray showed Charlotte Corday at the bar of the Revolutionary Tribunal, her wrists linked by a chain, addressing her judges, who listen in alarm as do the spectators and the two ruffians who guard her. The three judges sit on a throne inscribed "Vive La République," under a canopy decorated with cornucopias pouring out coins. Above them is a grotesque figure of Justice, holding scales and a dagger in place of her usual sword, trampling on a crown. The three judges, with animal-like features, are left to right: a barber, a comb sticking out of his pocket; a butcher, the most ferocious; a tailor, with scissors and a tape. Four ragged officials sit behind, all wearing legal wigs and Liberty Bonnets.

Between the judges and the accused lies the sprawling body of Marat, lying on a bed so short that his knees are bent upward. His body is covered with spots and shows a gaping wound. Beside it stand two men exhibiting evidence of the crime, one holding up a blood-stained shirt, the other a knife on a dish. This scene incorporated elements from Marat's funeral, which was orchestrated by the painter Jacques-Louis David, a friend of Marat and a

radical Jacobin himself. In the funeral procession Marat's body was carried on a wooden bedstead and his bloodied shirt exhibited on a pike.

Charlotte, a buxom young woman, gaily dressed with feathers in her hair, addresses the court defiantly:

Wretches, – I did not expect to appear before you – I always thought that I should be delivered up to the rage of the people, torn in pieces, & that my head, stuck on the end of of [*sic*] a pike, would have preceded Marat on his state-bed, to serve as a rallying point to Frenchmen, if there still are any worthy of that name. – But, happen what will, if I have the honours of the guillotine, & my clay-cold remains are buried, they will soon have conferred upon them the honours of the Pantheon; and my memory will be more honoured in France than that of Judith in Bethulia.

The words were those quoted in some English newspapers of the time, for example the *London Chronicle* on July 26, which were taken from a pamphlet published by Adam Lux, a German-speaking deputy from Mayenne, who was later guillotined himself.

The title of Gillray's print explains further that Corday appears "...at the bar of the Revolutionary Tribunal of Paris, July 17th 1793, for having rid the world of that monster of Atheism and Murder, the Regicide Marat, whom she Stabbed in a bath, where he had retired on account of Leprosy, with which, Heaven had begun the punishment of his Crimes — The noble enthusiasm with which this Woman met the charge, & the elevated disdain with which she treated the self created Tribunal, struck the whole assembly with terror & astonishment."   J.L.

JAMES GILLRAY
British, 1757-1815

15 *French-Telegraph making Signals in the Dark*   January 26, 1795
       (see p. 22)
(see p. 22)
BM 8612
Hand-coloured etching and aquatint on wove paper
25.0 x 35.5 cm
Gift of the Trier-Fodor Foundation, 1988
Acc. no. 88/109

This caricature was one of many that lampooned the parliamentarian Charles James Fox for his sympathetic attitude towards revolutionary France. Fox had broken with William Pitt who saw France as both a threat to British institutions and national security.

Gillray produced this satire in late January 1795 at a time when some Englishmen feared a French invasion. A French man, Claude Chappe, had recently invented a device for the visible transmission of messages. It consisted of a post at the top of which were pivotal arms. Different positions of the arms stood for different letters and numbers. A message could be relayed quickly from one post to another.

In this print this semaphore device is shown erected on the coast with the head of Fox on the top of the post. Although he is seen from the rear he can be seen looking to the right with a determined expression. His arms form those of the device. In his right hand he holds a lantern that lights the way for the French fleet, which is in full sail for England. In the background a French fort flies a tricoloured flag inscribed with the word "République." With his left hand he points downward to a dark cluster of roofs dominated by the dome of St. Paul's cathedral, obviously identifying the city of London.

The print suggests that Fox is a traitor to his own country. This allegation is reinforced by the circular brick structure at the base of the device in which an arched opening reveals a cache of daggers, evidently to be used for subversion.   J. L.

JAMES GILLRAY
British, 1757-1815

16 *Presages of the Millenium*   June 4, 1795
BM 8655
Wright 127
Hand-coloured etching and aquatint on wove paper
32.6 x 37.7 cm
Gift of the Trier-Fodor Foundation, 1982
Acc. no. 85/56

The French Revolution and the revolutionary wars that followed produced in some excited minds visions of the end of all time. One such visionary was the Englishman Richard Brothers who related his prophecies in pamphlets and in letters to the king, queen, and members of the government. He claimed to be a descendant of David and the Prince of the Hebrews and, as such, he demanded that the king surrender his crown to him. He denounced the war with France as being against a "chosen people" and prophesied the destruction of the royal family, parliament, and London. Eventually Brothers was imprisoned as a criminal lunatic and then transferred to a private asylum.

Gillray associated Brothers with the Foxites because they both opposed the war with France. In this print Pitt appears as Death riding naked on the White Horse of Hanover, galloping over the prostrate bodies of pigs, the swinish "Multitude." Pitt's body is emaciated, almost a skeleton, his flaming hair streams behind him encircled with a fillet inscribed "Destruction." In his right hand he brandishes a flaming sword and in his left holds a scaly monster with gaping jaws, webbed wings, and a serpent's tail.

Behind Pitt sits a naked imp wearing the feathered coronet of the Prince of Wales with the motto "Ich Di(en)" (I serve). He

grasps Pitt and kisses his posterior. In his left hand he holds out a paper: "Provision for the Millenium £125,000 pr anm." The horse's tail streams out, expanding into clouds and merging with the flames of Hell.

In the tail and flames are flying imps, representing various ministers, Dundas in the lead holding a pitchfork. Burke appears with webbed wings and a serpent's tail. In the foreground Pitt's opponents are being kicked towards Hell by the horse's hind legs. Fox himself has just been kicked in the face, and is staggering backward, clutching a document labelled "Peace." Wilberforce tumbles, holding his "Motion for a Peace." In falling, Fox pushes other Foxites into the flames.

The title continues: "with the Destruction of the Faithful, as Revealed to R. Brothers, the Prophet, & attested by M. B. Hallhead Esq./And e'er the Last Days began, I looked, & behold, a White Horse, & his Name who sat upon it was Death: & Hell followed after him; & Power was given unto him to kill with the Sword, & with Famine, & with Death; and I saw under him the Souls of the Multitude, those who were destroy'd for maintaing [*sic*] the word of Truth, & for the Testimony."   J. L.

JAMES GILLRAY
British, 1757-1815

17 *Promis'd Horrors of the French Invasion*   October 20, 1796
   (see p. 18)
BM 8826
Broadley, I, 94-96; app. 333, no. 736
Hand-coloured etching and aquatint on wove paper
32.0 x 44.0 cm
Gift of the Trier-Fodor Foundation, 1988
Acc. no. 88/107

This is one of the richest satires that Gillray did to alert the English to the danger posed by Revolutionary France. In the title the artist refers to Edmund Burke whose *Reflections on the Revolution in France* in 1790 had called attention to what he considered the pernicious implications of that event and had precipitated a split among the Whigs. The print was published in October 1796, soon after George III had warned parliament of the possibility of a French invasion and Prime Minister Pitt had proposed measures of defence. The Opposition had argued that the menace was illusory.

Gillray shows French troops marching up St. James's Street in London, the houses receding in perspective to the gate of the Palace, which is in flames. On the left and right are well-known clubs of the day, White's and Brookes's. The former is being raided by French troops. Members of the Opposition, sympathetic towards France, have occupied the latter triumphantly. In the centre of the street a Liberty Tree has been erected, a pole

Presages of the MILLENIUM; — with — The Destruction of the Faithful, — as Revealed to R:Brothers, the Prophet, & attested by M.B.Hallhead Esq.
"And eer the Last Days began, I looked, & behold, a **White Horse**, & his Name who sat upon it was **Death**: & **Hell** followed after him,; & Power was given unto him to kill with the
'Sword, & with **Famine**, & with **Death**; — And I saw under him the **Souls of the Multitude**, those who were destroy'd for maintaing the word of **Truth**, & for the Testimony

16 James Gillray, *Presages of the Millenium*, June 4, 1795

garlanded by flowers and capped by a Liberty Bonnet. To this pole Pitt has been tied, while Fox thrashes him ferociously. Between Fox's feet lies a headsman's axe.

Various eminent politicians can be identified. The ox on the right, from which hangs a broken cord, inscribed "Great Bedfordshire Ox," represents the Duke of Bedford. The ox tosses Burke in the air, who drops a couple of his recent pamphlets. Behind the ox, Lord Stanhope holds a pole to which is tied a pair of scales on which are balanced parts of the body of William Grenville, Pitt's foreign secretary. Stanhope looks up at the dismembered body with a satisfied smile. The Earl of Lauderdale, an opponent of the French wars, applauds him. In the background

English Jacobins advance, waving Liberty Bonnets.

Richard Sheridan, a playwright and politician who defended the French Revolution, enters the door of Brookes's with a triumphant smile. He wears a large porter's knot on his head and carries sacks that represent loot from the Treasury and the Bank of England. On the balcony over the door the Marquess of Landsdowne, who was one of the most consistently liberal statesmen of his day and one of the most unpopular, operates a guillotine. The purse of the Great Seal of England is tied to one of the posts of this machine. On the left corner of the balcony is a bowl containing, left to right, the heads of Lord Sydney, William Windham, and Pepper Arden, all "Killed off for the Public Good." In the

57

background stands Thomas Erskine, who had defended Thomas Paine's publication of the *Rights of Man* against a charge of sedition, holding up in triumph a firebrand composed of the Magna Carta. On the right corner of the balcony four other politicians watch the guillotine with satisfaction. On the doorpost below the French revolutionary hymn, the "Marsoiles" [*sic*] has been placed above "Rule Brit[annia]," which is torn.

Other horrors fill the street. In the foreground is a basket containing the head of Henry Dundas and a set of bagpipes labelled "To the care of Citizen Horne Tooke," who had attacked Dundas violently in a recent election. Beside it is a pile labelled "Waste Paper," including Acts of Parliament, the Bill of Rights, and Statutes. On the left grotesque goose-stepping French soldiers, led by a ferocious officer with a drawn sword, march past the severed head of Charles Richmond, whose paper on fortifying the coast lies nearby. One French officer tramples on a prostrate and bleeding body as he enters White's. Another officer transfixes the throat of a member. Some club members beg for mercy.

Some French soliders have reached the balcony above. They are using daggers and tossing bodies over the railing. The body of the Duke of York is being pushed over while the Prince of Wales is falling head first. The Duke of Clarence is about to be stabbed. The bodies of George Canning and Hawkesbury, tied back to back, hang from a lamp-bracket near the door. The lamp is surmounted by a broken crown.   J. L.

JAMES GILLRAY
British, 1757-1815

18 *Shrine at St. Ann's Hill*   May 26, 1798
BM 9217
Broadley, I, 114; app. 337, no. 804
Coll. de Vinck 4250
Aquatint on wove paper
36.5 x 26.3 cm
Gift of the Trier-Fodor Foundation, 1988
Acc. no. 88/110

Gillray continued to lampoon Fox for his support of the principles of the French Revolution and opposition to the war with France even after the latter had retired to Saint Ann's Hill. Fox is shown from the rear before an altar. His unpowdered hair is cropped. From his pocket protrudes a book labelled "New Constitut[ion]."

The altar is an un-Christian one. It is draped with a cloth on which crossed daggers are embroidered. On it is a guillotine, dripping blood. To this is tied a tricolour sash with two tablets, resembling those inscribed with the Ten Commandments that Moses brought down from Mount Sinai, but here inscribed with "Droit de l'Homme." Gillray presents the French Declaration of

18 James Gillray, *Shrine at St Ann's Hill,* May 26, 1798

the Rights of Man as a reversal of those prescribed by God:

I.   Right to Worship whom we please.
II. Right to create & bow down to any thing we chuse to set up.
III. Right to use in vain any Name we like.
IV. Right to work Nine Days in the Week, & do what we please on the Tenth.
V.   Right to honor both Father & Mother when we find it necessary.
VI. Right to Kill.
VII. Right to commit Adultery.
VIII. Right to Plunder.
IX. Right to bear what Witness we please.
X.   Right to covet our Neighbour['s] House and all that is his.

On the altar in front of the guillotine are three roughly made posts on rectangular pedestals, each bearing an inscription. The one in the centre, which replaces a crucifix, is inscribed "Exit Homo " instead of "Ecce Homo" ("Behold the Man," from *John* 19:5), and surmounted by a cap bearing the slogan "Egalité"; at its base is a skull and cross-bones. On the left-hand post, to which bleeding hands are nailed, is a bust of "Robert-speire" (Gillray's

EXHIBITION of a DEMOCRATIC-TRANSPARENCY, — with its Effect upon Patriotic Feelings;

Representing the Secret Committee throwing a Light upon the Dark Sketches of a Revolution found among the Papers of the Jacobin Societies lately apprehended, N.B. The Truth of the Picture is referred to the Consciences of the Swearers to the Innocence of O'Conner: And is Dedicated to the bosom-Friends of Fitzgerald; Quigley, Shears, Tone, Holt, & all other well-wishers to their Country

19 James Gillray, *Exhibition of a Democratic-Transparency*, April 15, 1799

spelling of Robespierre). The post on the left bears a bust of Bonaparte.

From the upper left a shaft of light surrounded by clouds shines down on Fox, a parody of divine light shining on a saint. Instead of little angels or putti are the winged heads of members of the Opposition, all wearing Liberty Bonnets and looking towards the "Droit de l'Homme." In front is Norfolk. Next to the left is Landsdowne with an enigmatic smile. They are followed by Bedford. Above him are Tierney and Lauderdale. Last is the malicious head of Nicholls. J. L.

JAMES GILLRAY
British, 1757-1815

19 *Exhibition of a Democratic-Transparency*   April 15, 1799
BM 9369
Wright 229
Hand-coloured etching and aquatint on wove paper
36.7 x 44.7 cm (imp.)
Gift of the Trier-Fodor Foundation, 1982
Acc. no. 82/244

Exhibition of a Democratic-Transparency was published in response to a report that was made by the Secret Committee to parliament in March 1799 in which it related its findings on the treasonable activities of secret societies in England and Ireland

(BM 9369). The fear of a revolution similar to that in France ran high at this time in England, and the conservative Pitt government made every effort to seek out and suppress potential insurrection. Freedom of speech had been taken away in 1795, and in 1799, the year of this caricature, the government invoked the Combination Acts which forebade the meeting of workers and employers (Herold, 222-223).

In this satire the Secret Committee of the House of Commons is seated around a table inspecting documents on revolutionary societies and clubs. The transparency hanging in front of the table is a large pictorial design illuminated from behind. Such transparencies were popular forms of street illumination; caricatures were frequently displayed in printshop windows as illuminations (Broadley, *Napoleon*, I, 338). The four images in this transparency reveal conjectured subversive intentions of revolutionary societies in England. Clockwise from the top left the pictures show members of the Opposition robbing the Bank of England, trying to murder the members of the government in the House of Commons, marching into St. James's Palace with French troops, and plundering the crown from the Tower of London. In the foreground members of the Opposition flee in terror, among them Charles Fox who holds his hand to his mouth, and Richard Sheridan who is the next on the right. The implication is that the Opposition harbours revolutionary aspirations (BM 9369).   A.J.

JAMES GILLRAY
British, 1757-1815

20 *French-Taylor, fitting John Bull with a "Jean de Bry"*   November 18, 1799
BM 9425
Wright 456
Hand-coloured etching on wove paper
36.4 x 26.4 cm (imp.)
Gift of the Trier-Fodor Foundation, 1985
Acc. no. 85/52

This caricature is a spoof on the extravagant French fashions that came into vogue after the fall of the Jacobins. A hideous French tailor wearing a long queue and the red bonnet of liberty fits a disgruntled John Bull, who is standing on a French book entitled *Nouveaux Costumes* into one of the latest French fashions, a Jean

20 James Gillray, *French-Taylor, fitting John Bull with a "Jean de Bry"*, November 18, 1799

de Bry jacket. This fashionable French jacket had a high collar, padded shoulders, and short coat tails (Cunnington, *Costume in Nineteenth Century*, 58) and was named after Jean-Antoine de Bry (1760-1834), a French politician and diplomat. While the French tailor promotes the ease, comfort, and "liberty" of the jacket, John Bull complains about the restriction and discomfort caused by its bulkiness.

Gillray's caricature also makes fun of the French Revolutionary government which, in 1795, had prescribed regulatory clothing for all government officials. The plaque on the back wall, near a picture that shows some of these uniforms, is ironically titled "Vive la Liberté" (BM 9425; Hill, *Satirical Etchings*, 119-120).   A.J.

Caricatures Parisiennes

Le Suprême Bonbon

Paris Chez Martinet, Libraire, Rue du Coq St Honoré

22 Anonymous (French), *Le Suprême Bon-bon* from *Caricatures Parisiennes,* c.1800

JAMES GILLRAY
British, 1757-1815

21 *The French-Consular-Triumverate*   January 1, 1800 (see p. 26)
BM 9509
Broadley, I, 132; app. 312, no. 362
Wright 250
Hand-coloured etching on wove paper
34.9 x 24.7 cm (imp.)
Gift of the Trier-Fodor Foundation, 1985
Acc. no. 85/55

Following the *coup d'état* of November 10, 1799 the three French consuls are drafting a new constitution – the fourth in a decade. Napoleon looks aggressive. Among the billowing feathers of Napoleon's exaggerated hat with immense plumage is an olive branch symbolic of his peace overture to George III. He dominates the meeting while the second and third consuls, Cambacérès on the left and Lebrun, on the right, merely bite their pens and stare sheepishly at the blank pages in front of them. Behind the table, the provisional second consul, Sieyès, pulls aside a curtain to reveal pigeon holes filled with constitutions of all types; and under the table firelit figures forge letters (BM 9509).

Signs of military despotism are everywhere: crossed guns above the curtain, Napoleon's long sword ironically named "Libertè," and Napoleon's oppressive boot trampling the Constitution of 1793. The bundle of papers in the middle of the table labelled "Constitution pour l'Avenir: Buonaparte Grande Monarque" foreshadows the Empire (Hill, *Mr. Gillray*, 126).   A.J.

ANONYMOUS
French, early 19th century

22 *Le Suprême Bon-bon* from *Caricatures Parisiennes*   c.1800
    (see p. 71)
    Hand-coloured etching on laid paper
    21.1 x 27.5 cm (imp.)
    Gift of the Trier-Fodor Foundation, 1986
    Acc. no. 85/453

In the early nineteenth century, as a result of Napoleon's policy of censorship, there were few political caricatures but many social satires. The materialistic bourgeoisie, who had made their fortune from speculation during the Revolution, became the butt of the satirist's venom. Exhausted by political change, society relished these caricatures on the manners and fashions of the *nouveaux riches* (Grand-Carteret, 69-93; Champfleury, 282).

Le Suprême Bon-bon is a take-off on a series of caricatures titled *Le Suprême Bon Ton*, a collection of thirty hand-coloured plates that recorded the clothing and customs of fashionable society in the early years of the nineteenth century (Colas). They satirized the social attitudes of the time without exaggerating or distorting the figures. Because the figures and costumes were rendered with remarkable accuracy, this series falls more into the category of fashion illustration than caricature.

Fashion is always a good barometer of a society's attitudes. The French fashions of the 1790s and early 1800s reflected society's veneration of Greece and Rome. Imitating the fashions of antiquity, French women donned white chemise dresses and sandals, and cut their hair short "à la Titus" (Laver, *Taste and Fashion*, 17, 20). Fashion of the early nineteenth century mirrored the general moral deterioration that occurred in France as people began to relax after the period of the Terror (Cunnington, *Costume in Nineteenth Century*, 12; Laver, *Taste and Fashion*, 18-19). Women paraded around in a state of "undress" (Angeloglou, 85): the diaphanous material of the Greek dresses revealed the absence of underclothing, the high slit in the skirt exposed the leg, and the dress was dampened so that it would cling to the body (Black, 233). In addition, the neckline fell daringly low, to the point where some women even went around bare-breasted (Laver, *Taste and Fashion*, 18-19).

23 Anonymous (French), *Le Suprême Bon Ton, No. 5* from *Caricatures Parisiennes*, c.1800

The figures in *Le Suprême Bon-bon* exhibit the fashionable Greek dresses, and the popular cashmere shawls and feathered turbans that came into vogue after Napoleon's expeditions abroad (Laver, *Taste and Fashion*, 22). An equally fashionable gentleman, sporting Hessian boots with tassels (Cunnington, *Costume in Eighteenth Century*, 233), offers bonbons – as a pun on "Bon Ton" – to several greedy ladies. On the table stand two jars bearing the names "huile devenus" (oil of Venus) and "elixir de longue vie" (elixir for long life). Health tonics and rare delicacies were in demand during this period when women frequently exhibited a green, sickly skin tone because of malnutrition (Angeloglou, 87).   A.J.

ANONYMOUS
French, early 19th century

23 *Le Suprême Bon Ton, No. 5* from *Caricatures Parisiennes*   c.1800
    Hand-coloured etching on laid paper
    20.5 x 30.5 cm (imp.)
    Gift of the Trier-Fodor Foundation, 1986
    Acc. no. 85/481

Famous in France during the late 1790s and early nineteenth century were the *Incroyables* and *Merveilleuses* (the "unbelievable ones" and the "marvellous ones"). These were members of the young, self-indulgent bourgeoisie who rebelled against the republican austerity of the period of the Terror. They showed their disdain by purposely cultivating a slovenly aristocratic manner (*Dictionnaire de l'Histoire de France Perrin*).

The *Incroyables* and *Merveilleuses* were well known for their outrageous outfits of violently contrasting styles and colours. The two gentlemen seated on the stools exhibit the typical attire of the *Incroyables*: messy hair, a huge neckcloth, a tiny waistcoat, pantaloons, and a gnarled wooden club (Laver, *Taste and Fashion*, 21; Cunnington, *Costume in Nineteenth Century*, 69-76). Some feigned an aristocratic elegance by wearing a powdered wig (although the wig had gone out of style with the Revolution) and by walking stooped with small steps (Robiquet, 122).

The *Merveilleuse* was the female counterpart to the *Incroyable*. She looked equally vain and ridiculous in her flimsy Greek dress. These dresses were not at all suitable for winter weather and, not surprisingly, many women fell ill with what was humorously called the "muslin disease." In fact, the Greek fashions of the period are said to have contributed to the increase of consumption (Boehn, *Modes and Manners*, I, 117). On the right a *Merveilleuse*, wearing long gloves, carries the popular parasol and a handbag known as a "réticule" – pockets in dresses had not come into use (Cunnington, *Costume in Nineteenth Century*, 369).

The group of *Incroyables* and *Merveilleuses* visit a shop where young boys, "décrotteurs" (boot scrapers) washed and polished boots with black varnish. Shoeblacks were ubiquitous in Paris on account of the muddy streets. Before Napoleon came to power, Paris lacked a sewage system, and carts were used to remove refuse from the streets while rain washed down the roads (Mercier, *Waiting City*, 52). Under Napoleon's leadership, five kilometres of sewers were built, reducing some of the inconvenience and odour (Robiquet, 64).   A.J.

ANONYMOUS
French, early 19th century

24 *Le Suprême Bon Ton, No. 7* from *Caricatures Parisiennes*   c.1800
Hand-coloured etching and stipple on laid paper
21.1 x 18.1 cm (imp.)
Gift of the Trier-Fodor Foundation, 1986
Acc. no. 85/482

With the goal of cleansing the country of Catholicism, some Revolutionaries in 1793-94 pursued a vigilant campaign to "dechristianize" the country. Priests and bishops were forced to resign their positions, the observance of the saints' days was forbidden, and religious symbols were destroyed. The Roman Catholic Church was replaced by pagan gods commemorating the ideals of the Revolution, the church of Notre-Dame became the "Temple of Reason," and huge festivals and parades were conducted to infuse people with the revolutionary spirit. Most churches, stripped of their valuable contents, became barracks,

24 Anonymous (French), *Le Suprême Bon Ton, No. 7* from *Caricatures Parisiennes*, c.1800

magazines, hospitals, or places of manufacturing (Lyons, 112; Rudé, 150; Broadley, *Journal of English Chaplain*, 157).

Dechristianization was not totally effective since the majority of the French population remained faithful to the Roman Church, and "removing" it merely forced religious practices to go underground. Indeed, some rural areas remained completely untouched by government policy (Lyons, 113-114). When Napoleon restored the Church in 1801, albeit in a much reduced state, many rejoiced. The ten-day working week of the Revolution was replaced by the seven-day week with Sunday as a day of rest, and the Gregorian calendar was reinstated (Cobban, 30). However, the bourgeoisie, who harboured anti-clerical sentiments, regarded the restoration of the Church more with suspicion and curiosity than with spiritual jubilation (Rudé, 238; Robiquet, 43). In fact, attending the newly restored services became a social event for fashionable society. Tickets could be purchased and seats reserved for some of the services, and orchestras were hired to entertain the fashionable congregations (Robiquet, 43).

Le Suprême Bon Ton, No. 7 portrays a group of fashionables at church. While the older generation demonstrates pious tendencies, the younger ones are distracted by more mundane interests.   A.J.

25 Anonymous (French), *Le Suprême Bon Ton, No. 8* from *Caricatures Parisiennes,* c.1800

ANONYMOUS
French, early 19th century

25 *Le Suprême Bon Ton, No. 8* from *Caricatures Parisiennes*   c.1800
Hand-coloured etching on wove paper
19.8 x 27.2 cm (imp.)
Gift of the Trier-Fodor Foundation, 1986
Acc. no. 85/483

Promenading on the arm of a gentleman, a fashionable lady flirts with the gentlemen around her. A wigged gentleman bows obsequiously: sexual overtones are suggested by the phallic walking cane held between his legs.

Napoleon has often been criticized for his reactionary attitude towards women. He blamed the moral laxity of the eighteenth century on the power of women, so when establishing his Empire he was careful to curb their influence (Herold, 121). Under the Civil Code the husband had full authority over the family. The Code also drastically tightened up the permissive divorce laws of the Directory — a woman could only sue for divorce if her husband installed his mistress in the family home (Rudé, 233) — and denied women the right to own or sell property (Herold, 121). Women were therefore completely dependent upon their husbands (Lyons, 65). They were expected to be good wives and mothers, and to confirm Napoleon's belief that "women should stick to knitting" (Herold, 121).

For the powerful women of the salons, like Madame Recamier, who were forced into arranged marriages to older men, Napoleon's Empire must have been terribly stifling to their political and social ambitions (Lyons, 66). It is small wonder that women were forced to resort to sex appeal in order to exert influence. An English visitor to France in 1814 wrote that "[women] are thus taught to make a parade of their sexual peculiarities...at the expense of their respectibility. They are taught to make the most of their influence as women, in order to gain for themselves and those connected with them, the mercenary ends which arise out of the competitions, hazards, designs, and necessities of daily life" (Scott, 195).   A. J.

ANONYMOUS
French, early 19th century

26 *Le Suprême Bon Ton, No. 9* from *Caricatures Parisiennes*   c.1800
Hand-coloured etching on laid paper
21.2 x 26.0 cm (imp.)
Gift of the Trier-Fodor Foundation, 1986
Acc. no. 85/484

Probably one of the best of the *Suprême Bon Ton* series, this print reveals the technical expertise of the fashion artist. The composition of the skaters creates a circular movement that guides the eye from the windblown figures in the foreground to the tumbling figure in the background. This swirling rhythm and pervading sense of cold and wind infuse this work with a dynamism lacking in most fashion plates.

Anglomania, the craze for English fashions and English manners, was originally generated by French diplomats and intellectuals returning from England. English ideas and customs found fertile soil in France where there was a strong desire to escape court convention and a yearning for the more simple and natural way of life supposedly found in England. Anglomania increased with the return of the *émigrés* after the fall of Robespierre, and by the end of the eighteenth century English customs had spread throughout France (Laver, *Taste and Fashion,* 15; Green, 30-36): there were English books, gardens, horses, carriages, and dogs. The French even dropped the rolled "r" in order to sound more English (Laver, *Taste and Fashion*, 15-16; Chapelle, 36-38).

This print illustrates some of the English fashions that were imported to France. On the left a gentleman wears the English riding coat called a "Garrick," named after the famous English actor. The lady wears a tailless jacket named after the eccentric Lord Spencer who, it is said, initiated this fashion when he burnt the tails of his coat standing by the fireplace, and after trimming the ends went out in public. English cloth, boots, bonnets, and shawls were also popular imports (Laver, *Taste and Fashion*, 15-16).

The sport of ice skating came to France from England in the eighteenth century. It immediately became a favourite pastime for the fashionable although the warm French climate did not permit a long skating season. When weather permitted, Parisians skated on the ponds in the Luxembourg and Tuileries gardens, on the lake in the Bois de Boulogne, or on the canal near Villette; they even went as far as Versailles to enjoy this sport (*Grand Dictionnaire Universal du XIXe Siècle*, XII, 395-396).   A. J.

Le Suprême Bon Ton, N.º 9.

à Paris chez Martinet libraire, Rue du Coq St Honoré

26 Anonymous (French), *Le Suprême Bon Ton, No. 9* from *Caricatures Parisiennes,* c.1800

JEAN-FRANÇOIS BOSIO
French, 1764-1827

27 *Bal de l'Opéra* from *Cinq Tableaux de costumes Parisiens*   1804
    (see colour plate on p. 39)
    Inventaire 19 s., III, 158
    Hand-coloured etching and engraving on wove paper
    27.5 x 49.5 cm (imp.)
    Gift of the Trier-Fodor Foundation, 1982
    Acc. no. 82/249

A popular artist of his time, Jean-François Bosio (1764-1827) executed lithographs and etchings of the fashions of the Salons. While some of his prints were published in the *Bon Genre* and *Suprême Bon Ton* series, his most famous work was a collection of

five prints published in 1804 under the title *Tableaux de costumes parisiens* (Beraldi; Delteil, 22; Arsène, 124). *Bal de l'Opéra* depicts the ball held annually at the Paris Opera when the pit was covered and given over to dancing. On one occasion, in 1805, Napoleon and Josephine attended the affair. Although they left early, the dancing continued until six in the morning (Simond, 109-111).

Bal de l'Opéra is typical of French satire of the early nineteenth century. Like Debucourt's *Promenade Publique*, Bosio's print is a lively rendering of the manners of Parisian society. It also reflects the attention to detail that was inherited from eighteenth-century French engraving. The grotesque distortion and exaggeration found in contemporary English caricature is largely absent in the subtle French satires of the early nineteenth century (Bornemann, 76).   A.J.

Le Bon Genre, N. 8.

Rue Montmartre N° 132.

28 Anonymous (French), *La Rencontre au Bal* from *Le Bon Genre, No. 8*, c.1805

ANONYMOUS
French, early 19th century

28 *La Rencontre au Bal* from *Le Bon Genre, No. 8*   c.1805
Hand-coloured etching and stipple on laid paper
20.7 x 25.5 cm (imp.)
Gift of the Trier-Fodor Foundation, 1986
Acc. no. 85/488

It has been claimed that the repercussion of any national catastrophe is "dancemania" and that at no other time was this more apparent than in the years following the Reign of Terror (Laver, *Taste and Fashion*, 18). By 1799, in Paris alone, there were 1,500 dance halls that housed public balls, private balls, and balls for every sector of society (Lyons, 64). This rage for dancing was a means of releasing the pent-up emotions accumulated during the years of political pressure.

Rencontre au Bal belongs to the popular *Le Bon Genre* series of hand-coloured fashion plates that recorded the fashions of the early nineteenth century (Holland, 57). This print portrays the variety of costumes worn at the numerous fancy dress balls which flourished at that time. Historical costumes, especially medieval dresses, were popular along with costumes from the Far East and Egypt (Laver, *Taste and Fashion*, 21-22 and 26-27). There was also a fad for women to dress up as men – note the figure in Turkish costume wearing a mask. The authorities tried to stop this trend, but to no avail (Blagdon, II, 247; Berry, II, 156).   A.J.

29 Anonymous (French), *Effets merveileux des bretelles*, c.1810

LES INVISIBLES EN TÊTE-A-TÊTE
Le Suprême Bon Ton N.º 16.

fig. 10   Anonymous, *Les Invisibles en tête-a-tête* from *Le Suprême Bon Ton N°. 16*, c.1815, engraving. By permission of the Bibliothèque Nationale, Paris.

ANONYMOUS
French, early 19th century

29 *Effets merveileux des bretelles*   c.1810
Hand-coloured etching and stipple on wove paper
24.4 x 32.7 cm (imp.)
Gift of the Trier-Fodor Foundation, 1986
Acc. no. 85/478

Effets merveileux des bretelles (The marvellous effects of suspenders) pokes fun at the fashion trends of the Empire. Much to the amusement of bystanders, a rotund gentleman is attached to a machine that pulls up his skin-tight breeches. Suspenders of cloth or ribbon had come into use at the end of the Consulate (1804), but it was not until 1811 that the first elastic suspenders were used (Boucher, 347).

The amused spectators on the right are themselves the butt of ridicule. The gentleman wears an oversized opera or cocked hat. These were fashionable during the Empire and could be folded and carried under the arm (Cunnington, *English Costume in Nineteenth Century*, 93). The lady wears an adaptation of the English straw bonnet called a "poke hat" (Wilcox). The brim of the "poke hat" became longer and wider during the early decades of the nineteenth century, providing a wonderful vehicle for satirists. The brim finally grew so long that its wearer was dubbed "l'invisible" because her face was completely obscured (Bigelow, 177). A caricature from the *Suprême Bon Ton* series, *No. 16*, shows several fashionable gentlemen with their heads concealed behind the bonnets of their elegant female companions (fig. 10).

There were a number of satirical prints published under the title *The Wonderful Effects of . . .* which implies there was probably a series aimed at ridiculing the fashions of the Empire. One humorous print, *The Wonderful Effects of tightening corsets* portrays a rotund woman hitched to a machine that pulls the strings

of her corset (reproduction in Bertuch, *Journal des Luxus*, III, inserted between 272 and 273).   A.J.

JAMES GILLRAY
British, 1757-1815

30 *A Phantasmagoria*   January 5, 1803 (see p. 68)
BM 9962
Broadley, app. 347, no. 968
Wright 272
Hand-coloured etching
35.5 x 25.8 cm (imp.)
Gift of the Trier-Fodor Foundation, 1981
Acc. no. 81/183

In this scene, which recalls Shakespeare's *Macbeth* (act 4, scene 1), three witches brew up a horrific vision of Britain during the Peace of Amiens (March 1802–May 1803). Prime Minister Henry Addington on the left throws money into the pot, while Foreign Secretary Lord Hawkesbury, kneeling on the right, feeds the fire with pieces of paper signifying English policies and land. Both are criticized for sacrificing Britain, her land and money, to appease Napoleon. A gruesome symbol of their self-interest is the decapitated lion of Britain whose paws and tail hang from the cauldron, and whose severed head in the foreground is surmounted by a Gallic cock. On the right stands a jubilant Charles Fox, who had recently met with Napoleon, and kneeling in the foreground, singing the Hymn of Peace, is William Wilberforce; both were supportive of maintaining peace with France.

The oval shape of this eerie scene set against a brick wall recreates the effect of a new device that was similar to a magic

Pub.d Jan.y 5th 1803. by J.Gillray. 27 St James's Street.

A PHANTASMAGORIA ; — Scene — Conjuring up an Armed-Skeleton.

30 James Gillray, *A Phantasmagoria,* January 5, 1803

lantern. Figures on gauze screens were projected on a wall. These ghost-like figures could be made to appear, diminish, or disappear. Coined "phantasmagoria" by M. De Philipsthal in 1802, the device became a common form of street entertainment (BM 9962; Hill, *Satirical Etchings*, 124).   A. J.

JAMES GILLRAY
British, 1757-1815

31 *L'Assemblée Nationale*   June 18, 1804 (see p. 70)
BM 10253
Broadley, I, 218; app. 293, no. 29
Hand-coloured etching
32.8 x 46.5 cm (paper)
Gift of the Trier-Fodor Foundation, 1981
Acc. no. 81/182

Gillray's *L'Assemblée Nationale* is, according to one scholar, "the most talented caricature that has ever appeared" (George Stanley, quoted in Hill, *Mr. Gillray*, 120). On one level, *L'Assemblée Nationale* purports to be a satire of the Opposition. Charles Fox (1749-1806), a prominent Whig politician, receives guests with his wife at their soirée, which is conducted in the French style. There are a number of references to Fox's sympathies with France in the caricature. On the wall, as part of the illumination, is an emaciated Napoleon in the guise of Atlas holding up the world, and on Mrs. Fox's fan there appears a picture of Napoleon. One interpretation of this caricature holds that Fox is the First Consul holding court after the execution of the king and the proclamation of the Republic (Hill, *Satirical Etchings*, 127; Hill, *Mr. Gillray*, 120). Of the three gentlemen bowing to the Foxes, the central figure is Lord Grenville with whom Fox was seeking to form a coalition government. Fox, therefore, bows to Grenville who looks subservient in response.

Gillray's print foreshadows the Regency. The health of King George III was in question at this time, and there was a great deal of speculation as to when the Prince of Wales would take the leadership. In the bottom right corner, bisected by the plate line, is the Prince of Wales with a quote from Shakespeare's *Henry IV, Part I* (act 1, scene 2) protruding from his pocket, which refers to his intention of abandoning a life of pleasure and leisure for one of work and responsibility when it suits his intentions. The portrait of George III, which hangs in shadow on the wall, and the painting on the right entitled "Worshipers of the Rising Sun" are glaring references to the ensuing Regency (Hill, *Satirical Etchings*, 127).

The Prince of Wales was normally an avid collector of Gillray's caricatures, but *L'Assemblée Nationale* so infuriated him that he offered to pay the artist to have the plate destroyed and the print suppressed. Although Gillray complied, he never received any money (Hill, *Mr. Gillray*, 120-121).   A. J.

ANONYMOUS
French, early 19th century

32 *Sauve qui peut, ou Les Anglais embarquant leur villes*   1803
(see p. 23)
BM 10147
Coll. de Vinck 7680
Hand-coloured etching and aquatint on laid paper
21.0 x 32.0 cm (imp.)
Gift of the Trier-Fodor Foundation, 1986
Acc. no. 85/489

Sauve qui peut (Run for your lives) makes fun of the English fear of an invasion of England by Napoleon's troops. In this satirical print the English are seen hurriedly boarding ships carrying their cities with them on stretchers in order to escape the feared attack by Napoleon. There were many French caricatures that portrayed the English as feeble and frightened. They acted as propaganda in France to bolster French morale (*Historical Dictionary of Napoleonic France*, 404-405; Holtman, 164-174).

Whether Napoleon actually intended to invade England is subject to debate. Nonetheless he made plans to invade and by the summer of 1804, there were 600-700 barges and a French army of 100,000 ready and waiting on the shores of Normandy. Although the plan for invasion was abandoned in 1805, Napoleon prolonged the threat in order to divert the British navy and force Britain to pour money into defence (*Historical Dictionary of Napoleonic France*, 172; Herold, 210; Cobban, II, 43).

The fear of Napoleon was real in England. There was a call to arms, nannies threatened mischievous children with stories of a fearsome Napoleon (Herold, 217), and a host of crude caricatures appeared vilifying the French invader (Hill, *Mr. Gillray*, 128). There were also many English caricatures envisioning ways in which Napoleon might invade, including balloon, bridge, and tunnel (Herold, 218).   A. J.

JAMES GILLRAY
British, 1757-1815

33 *The Grand Coronation Procession*   January 1, 1805 (see colour plate on pp. 40-41)
BM 10362
Broadley, I, 225; app. 315, no. 407
Coll. de Vinck 7948
Wright 294
Hand-coloured etching on laid paper
23.7 x 76.7 cm (imp.)
Gift of the Trier-Fodor Foundation, 1982
Acc. no. 82/246

Gillray's *Grand Coronation Procession* so brilliantly travesties the imperial pomp of Napoleon's coronation held on December 2,

L'ASSEMBLÉE NATIONALE, _or _Grand Cooperative Meeting at St. Ann's Hill. _ Respectfully Dedicated to the admirers of a Broad-Bottom'd Administration.

31 James Gillray, *L'Assemblée Nationale,* June 18, 1804

1804, that it is said the Emperor could not see the caricature without flying into a fit of anger (Hill, *Mr. Gillray*, 130).

Leading the procession is Prince Louis Bonaparte, one of Napoleon's brothers, who appears disconcerted by the fact that his son, who marches beside the rotund Mrs. Talleyrand, has been named Napoleon's heir apparent (BM, 10362). The three scantily clad ladies behind the prince are said to resemble Napoleon's sisters (BM, 10362). Behind his obese wife walks Foreign Minister Talleyrand-Périgord whose club foot was ridiculed here for the first time in caricature (BM, 10362). He carries Napoleon's family tree. Pope Pius VII appears to shrink, humiliated while a diabolic masked figure tries to seize the keys of St. Peter. The submissive stance of the Pope is symbolic of the secondary role that he played at the Coronation, where Napoleon refused to take communion or be consecrated in the traditional manner, and instead proceeded to crown himself Emperor (Herold, 134).

Napoleon appears meek and uncomfortable in the theatrical robes that were a recreation of those of Charlemagne (Schnapper,

219). On his red mantel are the faint outlines of bones and skulls. Josephine, who walks beside him, is so obese that she is completely unrecognizable. Her ladies in waiting are also grotesque: one lacks a nose while another has a black eye. Apparently Napoleon's sisters refused to carry Josephine's coronation mantle, and only after Napoleon threatened them with exile did they acquiesce. They took revenge during the ceremony when they gave the train a tug which caused Josephine to stumble (Herold, 134).

Behind Napoleon are the obsequious representatives of Holland, Spain, and Prussia, along with two rows of generals with their hands tied. Fouché, the minister of general police who had a reputation for being a terrorist, brandishes a bloody sword (Herold, 26). At the end of the procession various symbols are carried that refer to Napoleon's cruel policies and military despotism (BM 10362).

To legitimize his new authority Napoleon needed all the trappings of a king. The coronation was thus an extremely lavish and theatrical affair. Huge amounts of money were poured into coronation gowns; the church of Notre-Dame was redecorated; there were 140 horses in the procession, and 2,000 diamonds in Josephine's crown and diadem. The affair cost 8,500,000 francs (Laing, 132; Schnapper, 214). For all its pomp, the day itself was cold, windy, and wet, and the crowd that had been waiting since the early morning saw little of the three-hour ceremony (Schnapper, 220). The sausages and rolls sold to the onlookers hardly dispelled their disappointment (Herold, 134; Schnapper, 220).   A. J.

JAMES GILLRAY
British, 1757-1815

34 *Political Mathematician's, Shaking the Broadbottom'd Hemispheres*   January 9, 1807
BM 10697
Broadley, I, 225; app. 332, no. 717
Wright 336
Hand-coloured etching on wove paper
32.1 x 42.5 cm (comp.)
Gift of the Trier-Fodor Foundation, 1980
Acc. no. 80/44

The Ministry of Talents was a coalition government that had been formed in 1806 by Lord Grenville and Charles Fox. Although Fox died shortly afterward, the ministry was re-elected later that year (Webb, 144-145). This complex caricature presents the political situation after the re-election of the Ministry of Talents in November 1806.

In the centre of the caricature, sitting on a dunghill with mushrooms, cucumbers, cabbages, and thistles growing around it, is the Independent James Paull. In the large globes, representing Fox's old breeches, are the members of the Ministry of Talents who crowd around a table eating "loaves and fishes." The trifeathered emblem holding up the two globes is symbolic of the support the ministry received from the Prince of Wales. The continuation of this support was now in question since, with the death of Fox, the link with the Prince had been severed. On the right, trying to displace the ministry, are the Burdettites, the English Jacobins, and on the left, trying to bring down the Ministry, are the disciples of Pitt, the new Tory Opposition. In the foreground, rising from his newly dug grave, is Fox who looks disapprovingly upon the recent political developments (BM, 10697; Hill, *Fashionable Contrasts*, 157-158).

The Ministry of Talents was unpopular, owing largely to Gillray's vehement caricatures (George, *English Caricature 1793-1832*, 88). Indeed it was the first time Gillray had engaged in outright criticism of the government, and "seldom could he have worked to greater political effect than against the Talents" (Hill, *Mr. Gillray*, 113). He portrayed the Talents as divided and

34 James Gillray, *Political Mathematician's, Shaking the Broadbottom'd Hemispheres,* January 9, 1807

competing for power; their political self-interest, he claimed, was placing England in danger of an invasion from France (George, *English Caricature 1793-1832*, 98). Napoleon is visible in the background of this caricature, looming over the Channel with a telescope to his eye observing the chaos and vulnerability of Britain. Although the Ministry of Talents was not very popular, its one great accomplishment was the abolition of slavery in 1807 (Webb, 144-145).   A. J.

JAMES GILLRAY
British, 1757-1815

35 *Very Slippy Weather*   February 10, 1808 (see p. vi)
BM 11100
Broadley, app. 341, no. 864
Wright 559
Hand-coloured etching on wove paper
25.7 x 19.9 cm (imp.)
Gift of the Trier-Fodor Foundation, 1985
Acc. no. 85/43

In *Very Slippy Weather*, a group on the street inspect the caricatures hanging in the window of Hannah Humphrey's print shop in London. Inside the shop two gentlemen peruse a caricature titled *Catholic Emancipation* (BM, 11100). Gillray's caricature is based on a sketch made by a friend and patron of the artist, Reverend John Sneyd. Sneyd had executed a series of sketches on the effects of various weather conditions (Hill, *Fashionable Contrasts*, 137). Hannah Humphrey's print shop was exclusive. It was one of the few places in London that attracted the patronage of "upper class people with taste and knowledge" (Hill, *Fashionable Contrasts*, 8). "Mrs" Humphrey owed her success to Gillray. She and Gillray had formed a partnership in 1791 that granted the Humphrey establishment the enviable prestige of selling Gillray's work (Hill, *Mr. Gillray*, 38). Although Gillray was supposed to produce prints only for Mrs Humphrey, he surreptitiously sold them to other dealers (Broadley, *Napoleon*, I, 56).

From 1793 to 1815, when he died insane, Gillray lived above Mrs Humphrey's print shop. It was a particularly agreeable situation for the artist because it guaranteed comfort and regular meals. It is said that the relationship between Gillray and Mrs Humphrey, an unmarried woman fifteen to twenty years older than Gillray, went beyond professional interests. Although they never married, Gillray reportedly proposed to her on several occasions (Hill, *Mr. Gillray*, 38-40).

Print shops catering to the upper classes had become quite lucrative by the late eighteenth century (Jouve, *L'Age d'Or*, 44). Seventy-one print shops in London produced 8000 prints between 1770 and 1815 (Hill, *Satirical Etchings*, XVI). The clientele viewed the prints in the comfort of lounges and could rent folios for an evening's entertainment (Brown University, 10). Coloured prints were sold for two to three shillings while plain ones cost one or two shillings (Jouve, *L'Age d'Or*, 42). Such prices placed prints beyond the reach of the working class since an unskilled labourer was fortunate to earn as much as ten shillings a week (Hill, *Fashionable Contrasts*, 23). Nevertheless prints were hung in the windows of print shops and posted on tavern walls so that everyone might enjoy them (Jouve, *L'Age d'Or*, 42). Gillray was a particular favourite. When a new Gillray caricature was placed on display in the window of Hannah Humphrey's shop a "veritable madness" occurred, and "you had to make your way through the crowds with your fists" (Hill, *Fashionable Contrasts*, 6).   A.J.

ANONYMOUS
French, early 19th century

36 *L'Elégant chez son marechal ferrant* from *Le Suprême Bon Ton, No. 21*   February 1812
   BE 20: (February 15, 1812), 238, no. 263
   Hand-coloured etching and stipple on laid paper
   20.3 x 26.0 cm (imp.)
   Gift of the Trier-Fodor Foundation, 1986
   Acc. no. 85/525

In *L'Elégant chez son maréchal ferrant* (The elegant at the blacksmith's), a gentleman kneeling on a cane stool awaits the blacksmith. It was the fashion of the time to wear high-heeled boots with horse shoes (Bertuch, *Journal des Luxus*, III, 386-387).   A.J.

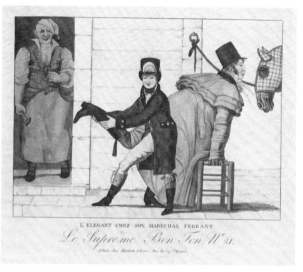

36 Anonymous (French), *L'Elégant chez son marechal ferrant* from *Le Suprême Bon Ton, No. 21,* February 1812

ADRIEN VICTOR AUGER
French, b. 1787
Etching by ALPHONSE HÛ

37 *La Chinoise de Province et son Magot, ou le Bon Goût transplanté*
   December 1813/1814
   BE 50: (December 10, 1813), 546, no. 737
   Inventaire 19 s., I, 231
   Etching and engraving on laid paper
   41.5 x 27.8 cm (sheet)
   Gift of the Trier-Fodor Foundation, 1985
   Acc. no. 85/50

The signature "V Auger delin" in the bottom left corner of this satire indicates that this print was made after a sketch by Adrien Victor Auger. Of the engraver, Alphonse Hû, who actually made the print, little is known. This is a print of exceptional quality which rivals Bosio's *Bal de l'Opéra* (cat. no. 27) in its attention to detail. From the pagoda-like awnings in the background to the delicate pattern on the gentleman's stockings, this caricature is filled with colourful patterns and textures.

In this print, two visitors from the country – "La Chinoise," referring to the fashion for things Chinese, and "son magot," meaning a grotesque figurine – inspect theatre announcements on a wall in Paris. They wear the lavish fashions of the late Empire.

The elaborate and colourful clothing in this work is indicative of the changes in female fashion towards the end of the Empire. As textile production advanced, heavier materials such as silk, satin, taffeta, and velvet took the place of the flimsy muslin of the Greek fashion. Dresses were shorter and more elaborately embellished with trimmings, frills, and flounces. The waistline was high

37 Adrien Victor Auger and Alphonse Hû, *La Chinoise de Province et son Magot, ou le Bon Goût transplanté*, December 1813/1814

and remained so until 1817 (Ginsburg, *Four Hundred Years*, 35; Cunnington, *Costume in Nineteenth Century*, 371). A sausage roll bustle tied under the bust hid the natural figure and made the dress flair out, provoking one English observer to comment that a woman dressed in this fashion resembled "a large bell of which the two shuffling feet look like the double clapper" (Scott, 100). A.J.

ANONYMOUS
French, late 18th century

38 *Le désarroi*   September 1814 (see colour plate on p. 44)
BF 38: (September 24, 1814), 278, no. 650
Hand-coloured etching on laid paper
29.8 x 24.2 cm (sheet)
Gift of the Trier-Fodor Foundation, 1982
Acc. no. 82/252

The chaos or confusion in this caricature is caused by an accident in which a horse-drawn carriage carrying an English officer and his wife collides with a ladder from which an artist is painting a sign on the front of a wine merchant's store.

This work comments on the dangers of the Paris streets. Before the Revolution, private carriages sped along the narrow roads at breakneck speeds, and there were no sidewalks to protect pedestrians. Accidents were frequent and took at least two hundred lives a year (Mercier, *Picture of Paris*, 134). Drivers were never held responsible; while the carriage drove off, the victim was left abandoned in the road (Mercier, *Picture of Paris*, 14). The habit of placing straw in the road to blunt the sound of hooves and wheels led to further problems. Not only did it give off a pungent odour and make a mess, it also prevented pedestrians from hearing approaching vehicles (Mercier, *Waiting City*, 232).

During the Revolution, private carriages all but disappeared. Armorial decorations and livery fell out of use. After the turbulence of the Revolution visitors in Paris noted a small increase of carriages in the streets, especially in the number of public coaches (Blagdon, I, 14). The new sleek carriages, imported from England, were lighter, higher, noisier, and much faster (Mercier, *Picture of Paris*, 237). To protect pedestrians, authorities set down safety precautions: bells had to be attached to the horse's neck, two lights had to be lit at night, and heavy fines were levied on reckless drivers (Blagdon, II, 552-553). Although some visitors found the streets of post-Revolutionary Paris safer and more convenient, there were still others who thought otherwise: "…like lightening [*sic*] [carriages] pass; and in consequence the pedestrian is no more than grass or paving-stone…" (Mercier, *Picture of Paris*, 237).   A.J.

39 Thomas Rowlandson, *The Corsican Toad under a Harrow*, November 27, 1813

THOMAS ROWLANDSON
English, 1756-1827

39 *The Corsican Toad under a Harrow*   November 27, 1813
BM 12104
Broadley I, 341; app. 305, no. 237
Coll. de Vinck 8841
Grego, II, 259
Hand-coloured etching
23.3 x 33.6 cm (comp.)
Gift of J. T. Johnson, 1981
Acc. no. 81/241

In November 1813, the Allies were closing in on France; their peace initiative having been thwarted by Napoleon, they planned to invade in January 1814 (Markham, 138-139; Cobban, II, 62).

This satire, attributed to Rowlandson, shows the Allies taking their revenge on Napoleon. They draw a harrow over the prostrate Emperor who cries out with pain. Pulling on the first rope from right to left are Britain, Sicily, and Spain, and on the second are Prussia, Sweden, and Austria. Giving Napoleon an extra prod is a Russian Cossack, and sitting on top of the harrow is a pensive Dutchman (Broadley, *Napoleon*, I, xiv; BM 12104).   A.J.

THOMAS ROWLANDSON
British, 1756-1827

40 *The Devils Darling*   March 12, 1814 (see p. 31)
BM 12196
Broadley, I, 342; app. 308, no. 276
Coll. de Vinck 7814
Grego, II, 278
Hand-coloured etching on wove paper
34.8 x 24.8 cm (imp.)
Gift of the Trier-Fodor Foundation, 1982
Acc. no. 82/241

Napoleon was frequently associated by satirists with supernatural forces and demonic spirits (Hill, *Mr. Gillray*, 128). In this satire Napoleon is presented as the very incarnation of evil, the Devil's own progeny. A grinning devil cradles the Emperor who is wrapped in a tricoloured blanket. From the devil's hand hangs the medal of the Legion of Honour. The original idea for Rowlandson's famous caricature came from a German print that was widely copied throughout Europe and England in different sizes and formats (Langle, 181, with reproduction).   A.J.

ANONYMOUS
British, early 19th century
after JOHANN MICHAEL VOLTZ (1784-1858)

41   *Napoleon...Make Peace With!!!*   March/April 1814   (see p. 25)
BM 12202
Broadley, II, 242-257; app. 327, no. 626
Hand-coloured etching on wove paper
46.2 x 28.2 cm (sheet)
Gift of the Trier-Fodor Foundation, 1987
Acc. no. 86/273

Napoleon...Make Peace With!!! is an English version of a famous German caricature by Voltz titled *Triumph des Jahres 1813.* Voltz's caricature is a hieroglyphic portrait of Napoleon that recalls the fantastic heads composed of fruit and vegetables by the Milanese painter Giuseppe Arcimboldo (1527-1593) (fig. 11) (Bornemann, 107). Published January 1, 1814, Voltz's provocative image of Napoleon was intended to incite the Germanic states to revolt against Napoleon (Broadley, *Napoleon*, II, 244). The English print shop owner Rudolph Ackermann happened to be in Germany at the time of the publication of Voltz's satire, he witnessed the immense popularity of the print and quickly had it reproduced in London on a larger scale in the form of a broadsheet. He also changed the German inscription to give the print more English appeal (Broadley, *Napoleon*, II, 246).

The inscription on the German print explains that Napoleon's hat is composed of the Prussian eagle that has seized Napoleon and will not let him go; his face is composed of all the dead bodies that lusted after power; his neck is a sea of blood and his coat is a map of the dissolved states of the Confederation of the Rhine. The cities on the map are those in which Napoleon lost battles. The epaulette is the hand of God reaching down to seize the spider situated over the heart, which has ensnared the Germanic States in its web (BM 12177; Broadley, *Napoleon, II*, 244-245).

The English print alters this imagery slightly. Instead of the Prussian eagle, the hat now represents a French eagle which has been maimed, while the epaulette symbolizes the Allies. A lettered ring on each finger signifies the countries that have rallied to free the enslaved Germanic states (BM 12202). The legend contains a long list of satirical titles that accuse Napoleon of many acts

fig. 11   Giuseppe Arcimboldo, *L'Été (Summer)*, 1573; oil on canvas, 76.5 x 64.0 cm.
By permission of the Musée du Louvre, Paris.

of cruelty. One accusation that appeared repeatedly in English anti-Napoleonic satire was Napoleon's apparent inhumanity at Jaffa. The title *"Inventor of the Syrian Method. . ."* refers to Napoleon's capture of the city of Jaffa in March 1799 during the Syrian Campaign. Napoleon is reported to have massacred several thousand Turkish prisoners and to have given arsenic to his troops who had been infected with the plague. It was said that food supplies had run out, that there was no way of feeding and looking after the Turkish prisoners, and arsenic was a humane way of easing the soldiers' long painful death (Herold, 59; BM 10663, 10662).

Voltz's image of Napoleon was reproduced all over Europe: in Spain, Holland, Germany, England, and even in France. What made this work so important was the fact that it was the first European caricature to equal the brilliance of the English Napoleonic satires. Between 1798 and 1815 the caricatures of Gillray, Rowlandson, and Cruikshank had been reproduced in smaller formats and distributed throughout Europe (Broadley, *Napoleon*, II, 103).

Although Continental caricaturists were aware of English satire, the political situation had prevented them from mirroring it. With the demise of Napoleon, artists like Voltz could finally pay tribute to the English artists who had stood alone in their war with Napoleon (Broadley, *Napoleon*, II, 244).   A.J.

ANONYMOUS
French, late 18th century

42 *Buonaparte au Bain*   Spring 1814 (see colour plate on p. 42)
Broadley, II, 53; app. 360, no. 36
Hand-coloured etching on laid paper
27.2 x 36.3 cm (imp.)
Gift of the Trier-Fodor Foundation, 1982
Acc. no. 82/255

Jean-Baptiste Isabey's famous print of 1792 entitled *The Little Coblentz* provided the first glimpse of Napoleon in French caricature. In it Napoleon was hardly visible standing among the fashionable figures strolling along a Paris street (Broadley, *Napoleon*, II, 33). Not until his fall did Napoleon appear again in French caricature. Stringent censorship laws during the Consulate and the Empire led to the reduction in the number of Paris newspapers from 73 in 1800 to 4 in 1811 and curtailed any criticism of Napoleon (*Historical Dictionary of Napoleonic France*, 403; Holtman, 166).

Following Napoleon's humiliating military defeats in Russia and the economic hardships imposed by the Continental system (Cobban, II, 62), censorship alone was incapable of repressing the growing discontent in France. French anti-Napoleonic caricatures began to appear in 1813. Cautious at first, they soon escalated in both vehemence and number, so that by the beginning of 1814 there was a veritable flood of caustic caricatures attacking Napoleon (Broadley, *Napoleon*, II, 50, 52).

Of this spate of French satires, *Buonaparte au Bain* stands out as "one of the finest caricatures of the period" (Broadley, *Napoleon*, II, 53). It presents a rare view of a naked Napoleon seated in a glass-sided bathtub composed of the Bonaparte and French mantles. While a stern Napoleon turns on the taps from which flow the tears and blood of France, the "ange du nord," possibly England, offers a tearful France the lillies and olive branch of peace.

It is certainly an eloquent appeal for peace from a country that was exhausted by war. Towards the end of the Napoleonic Wars, there was open resistance to Napoleon's now ruthless manner of raising conscripts (Cobban, II, 62). Many tried to evade the draft by fleeing or maiming themselves, and as married men did not have to fight, many escaped war by marrying (Herold, 143). In total, 860,000 men between the ages of 23 and 44 died in Napoleon's military expeditions, half of them under the age of twenty-eight (Cobban, II, 66).   A.J.

GEORGE CRUIKSHANK
British, 1792-1878

43 *Snuffing Out Boney!*   May 1, 1814 (see p. 28)
BM 12254
Broadley I, 361; app. 337, no. 811
Cohn 1992
Coll. de Vinck 8837
Etching (coloured impression) on wove paper
35.4 x 25.6 cm (imp.)
Gift of the Trier-Fodor Foundation, 1980
Acc. no. 80/41

"I was cradled in caricature," declared George Cruikshank (Wardroper, 8). This hardly comes as a surprise since Cruikshank, the son of a well-known caricaturist in London, spent his childhood haunting his father's workshop (Wardroper, 7). For a short period, Cruikshank pursued a career in acting but he eventually returned to caricature and to his father's profession (Wardroper, 11). One of his first tasks as an apprenticing caricaturist in 1811 was to complete the unfinished plates left by the then insane Gillray. For this reason, and partly because of the intense political situation at this time, Cruikshank's early work is composed largely of political satire (Bates, 11). Cruikshank was extremely productive: by 1813, his production had exceeded that of his contemporaries, including the prolific Rowlandson (Wardroper, 14).

Snuffing Out Boney! is a satire on Napoleon's downfall. Published May 1, 1814, Cruikshank's work coincided with the signing of the Peace of Paris, which restored the Bourbon monarchy in France and officially ended Napoleon's rule. In this satire an elated Russian Cossack snuffs out a shrieking mouse-sized Napoleon who stands in a candle holder. In the picture on the back wall, a Cossack places an outsized snuffer over a diminutive Napoleon. This caricature probably drew inspiration from the many English caricatures that appeared at the end of Napoleon's unsuccessful campaign in Russia. Among these satires was a caricature by William Elmes called *The Cossack Extinguisher* from November 1813, in which a smiling Cossack places his fur hat, in the shape of an extinguisher, over a puny Napoleon (Broadley, *Napoleon*, I, 325, with reproduction).

Napoleon often appeared in English satire as "Little Boney," a dwarf figure. This image of the fearsome leader reduced to lilliputian stature was created by Gillray in 1803, at the height of the invasion scare in England, and was a visual means of undermining Napoleon's omnipotence (Bornemann, 95; Hill, *Mr. Gillray*, 127).   A.J.

44 Anonymous (French), *Vive le Roi!…ou Les Spéculateurs et les Politiques en défaut,* May 4, 1814

ANONYMOUS
French, early 19th century
Etching by ALEXIS-JOS MILLET
French, b. 1790

44 *Vive le Roi!… ou Les Spéculateurs et les Politiques en défaut*
    May 4, 1814
BF 16 and 17: (May 21, 1814), 108, no. 164
Broadley, app. 378, no. 316
Coll. de Vinck 9055
Hand-coloured etching on laid paper
21.5 x 17.6 cm (image)
Gift of the Trier-Fodor Foundation, 1986
Acc. no. 85/490

The three men reading the announcements of Louis XVIII's return on a wall in Paris represent the conflicting responses to the news

of Napoleon's fall. There is the overjoyed royalist who hails the king with a jubilant cheer, the humiliated Bonapartist with the long nose who reads a denigrating poster titled "Ode sur le chûte du Tyrant" (Ode to the fall of the tyrant), and the distressed speculator who carries in his pocket "Essai sur Le Sucre de Betteroy" (An essay on sugar-beet) (Coll. de Vinck, 9055).

The Continental System, which Napoleon instituted in 1806, was intended to destroy England economically and establish France as the leading economic power on the Continent. However, it had the adverse effect of starving France of raw materials, and efforts were made to remedy this without trading with England (Markham, 105-107). Sugar-beets, chicory, and rapeseed were used as substitutes for imported cane sugar and coffee, but for the most part they proved unsuccessful (Coll. de Vinck 9515; Palmer, 96).

The return of the Bourbon monarchy signified the end of the Continental System, thus bringing to a close a period of intense wartime opportunism and speculation (*Historical Dictionary of Napoleonic France*, 131-132; Coll. de Vinck 9515). The speculator in this caricature is horrified by the news of Louis XVIII's impending return, since it marks the end of his monopoly of the sugar-beet trade in France.   A.J.

ANONYMOUS
French, early 19th century

45 *Les Milords Pouffes à Paris, ou la famille Anglaise du Suprême Bon ton de Londres*   September 1814 (see p. 88)
BF 36 and 37: (September 17, 1814), 266, no. 636
BM 12357
Hand-coloured etching on wove paper
23.0 x 31.4 cm (imp.)
Gift of the Trier-Fodor Foundation, 1986
Acc. no. 85/524

The periods of peace between England and France encouraged upper-class English tourists to flock to France. In 1802 alone, during the Peace of Amiens, there were 10,000 British visitors in Paris (Maxwell, 212). These English tourists were eager to see the treasures in the Louvre that had been plundered during the Napoleonic Wars. They were also curious to see the changes made by the Revolution and to enjoy the amusements of the boulevards and the Palais-Royal (George, *Hogarth to Cruikshank*, 146; Chapelle, 44-45).

An English chaplain visiting Paris in 1801 wrote, "All people seem to be fond of the English" (Broadley, *Journal of English Chaplain*, 86). How wrong he was! In 1802 English visitors were

LES MILORDS POUFFES à PARIS, OU LA FAMILLE

Les Milords Pouffes à Paris, ou la famille Anglaise du Suprême Bon ton de Londres.

45 Anonymous (French), *Les Milords Pouffes à Paris, ou la famille Anglaise du Suprême Bon ton de Londres,* September 1814

merely laughed at; after 1815, they were despised. The removal of the treasures from the Louvre, and the presence of Allied soldiers in Paris, made the humiliation of defeat very real for the French (Maxwell, 270). They vented their frustration in vicious caricatures that ridiculed the English (George, *Hogarth to Cruikshank,* 211). Ironically, these prints were inspired by English caricatures that had slipped into France during the Empire (Jouve, *L'Age d'Or,* 48; Broadley, *Napoleon,* II, 50).

Les Milords Pouffes à Paris (My lords guffaw in Paris) shows several English visitors meeting unexpectedly on a street in Paris. These crudely rendered figures are typical of the way in which the English were satirized by the French: the gentlemen were invariably presented as obese John Bull-like figures, wearing overly long coat-tails and flowerpot hats, while the ladies were shown with protruding teeth (BM 12357; George, *Hogarth to Cruikshank,* 211). Ironically, these ruthless satires were tolerated by the English during a period of military occupation (George, *Hogarth to Cruikshank,* 211). A.J.

HENRI GERARD-FONTALLARD
French, b. c.1798

46 *Anglais à la Promenade* September 1814
BF 36 and 37: (September 17, 1814), 263, no. 551
BM 12365
Inventaire 19 s., IX, 43, no. 2
Hand-coloured etching on laid paper
26.8 x 18.8 cm (imp.)
Gift of the Trier-Fodor Foundation, 1986
Acc. no. 85/517

During the lull in hostilities between the two countries following the short-lived Treaty of Amiens in 1803, French caricatures of the English had been mostly political; after Napoleon's exile to Elba in April 1814 and again after his defeat at Waterloo in June 1815 the caricatures were predominantly social. French artists produced a flood of prints satirizing their rivals' alleged bad taste in clothes, their lack of refinement in eating, their corpulent

ANGLAIS À LA PROMENADE

Dignié à la Direction de la Librairie &c.

46 Henri Gerard-Fontallard, *Anglais à la Promenade,* September 1814

physiques, and lack of delicacy in relations with the fairer sex.

In this caricature the artist depicts two English men promenading impassively in single file, the haughty one in the lead providing an amusing contrast to the one following in his footsteps. The taller one wears a flowerpot hat, very high stock and frilled shirt, a coat with long narrow tails and a collar that projects from his shoulders, and tight trousers slit up the ankle for several inches, the edges of the slit lined with buttons which are unfastened. An eyeglass on a ribbon hangs from his neck. He has carefully curled false whiskers. The stout chubby man following along is a young midshipman, wearing a high-crowned hat, a short jacket, and wide trousers.   J. L.

LOUIS-FELIX LEGENDRE
French, b. 1794

47 *Les Anglais au Salon de 1814*   November 2, 1814 (see p. 34)
BF 45: (November 12, 1814), 346, no. 772
Coll. de Vinck 9282
Inventaire 19 s., XIII, 314, no. 2
Hand-coloured etching on wove paper
25.8 x 29.5 cm (imp.)
Gift of the Trier-Fodor Foundation, 1986
Acc. no. 85/523

Among the paintings on view in the Salon of November 1814 were Girodet's *Le Déluge* (fig. 12), Gros's *Charles XV à St Denis,* Guerin's *Phèdre* and Prud'hon's *La Justice et la Vengeance divine pour suivant le crime.* These early Romantic paintings had already been exhibited during the Empire, but for the sake of the foreigners who came to Paris after the war, they were presented once again (Chapelle, 97; Coll. de Vinck, 9282).

Louis-Félix Legendre's caricature, published the day before the opening of the Salon in November 1814, anticipates the boorish behaviour of English tourists in front of works of art, which were already greatly respected and praised in France. Crowded together in the Salon, the English tourists gawk at the paintings, their faces register shock, disgust, and boredom. In fact, a large group of English tourists did attend the exhibit and seemed genuinely interested and even moved by what they saw (Chapelle, 97; Coll. de Vinck 9282).   A.J.

fig. 12   A. L. Girodet-Trioson, *Le Déluge,* 1806; oil on canvas, 4.31 x 3.41 m. By permission of the Musée du Louvre, Paris.

AMUSEMENTS DES ANGLAIS A LONDRES

don, II, 558).

French caricatures provide an unflattering portrait of English tourists who are often shown as unruly, drunken oafs. In this scene, a group of disorderly English visitors skate on the Canal de l'Ourcq, located in the small town of Villette on the north-east perimeter of Paris. The canal was built during the Empire and Restoration as a means of increasing the water supply to Paris (Hillairet, I, 14-15; *Dictionnaire de Paris*, 572-573; *Grand Dictionnaire Universal*, XI, 1571). Compared to the grace of the skaters in *Le Suprême Bon Ton, No. 9* (cat. no. 26), the English appear awkward and clumsy.   A. J.

ANONYMOUS
French, early 19th century

50 *Le Thé Anglais*   January 1815 (see p. 32)
BF 3: (January 21, 1815), 48, no. 63
Hand-coloured etching and stipple engraving on blue laid paper
25.5 x 35.0 cm (sheet)
Gift of the Trier-Fodor Foundation, 1986
Acc. no. 85/468

In *Le Thé Anglais*, several English ladies chat with a rather affected English officer while they are served tea. They exhibit the conservative style of dress with the low waistline which the French women found so prudish (George, *Hogarth to Cruikshank*, 211) (see Auger, *La Chinoise de Province et son Magot, ou le Bon Goût transplanté* [cat. no. 37] for typical French fashion around 1815). The setting for the tea party is austere, and the tone sombre, communicating the French conception of the solemn English.

The English tradition of drinking tea came to France in the 1790s (Grand-Carteret, 75). The English tradition became so popular that, by 1802, it had replaced the French evening meal. After an evening at the theatre, one dined on English sandwiches, cake, punch, and tea (Blagdon, I, 210-214).   A. J.

ANONYMOUS
French, early 19th century

48 *Amusements des Anglais à Londres*   November 1814
BF 47: (November 26, 1814), 369, no. 809
BM 12353
Hand-coloured etching on wove paper
19.1 x 27.1 cm (imp.)
Gift of the Trier-Fodor Foundation, 1986
Acc. no. 85/465

In *Amusements des Anglais à Londres*, the English are portrayed reading morbid literature (Young's *Night Thoughts*), drinking too much beer, and commiting suicide. This graphically expresses the French belief that the English were obsessed with death and came to France to escape *ennui* (George, *Hogarth to Cruikshank*, 211).   A. J.

ANONYMOUS
French, early 19th century

49 *Les Anglais au Canal de L'Ourc*   January 25, 1815 (see colour plate on p. 43)
Coll. de Vinck 9283
Hand-coloured etching on laid paper
26.0 x 34.6 cm (imp.)
Gift of the Trier-Fodor Foundation, 1986
Acc. no. 85/469

The behaviour of English tourists in France was not always admirable. English travel diaries tell of ostentatious, pleasure-seeking tourists (Maxwell, 31) who "appear to glory in...astonishing the natives with the eccentricity of their behaviour" (Blag-

ANONYMOUS
French, early 19th century

51 *Les Petits-Maîtres anglais*   October 20, 1815
Coll. de Vinck 9271
Hand-coloured etching and stipple on laid paper
30.4 x 20.9 cm (imp.)
Gift of the Trier-Fodor Foundation, 1986
Acc. no. 85/471

"Petits-maîtres" was a term originally applied by the English to the French in the eighteenth century. It was a derogatory name for a man with an affected, judgemental manner, and an inflated sense of his own importance (Duffy, 36 and 51). This term was

Les Petits-Maîtres anglais.

51 Anonymous (French), *Les Petits-Maîtres anglais,* October 20, 1815

thrown back at the English when, at the end of the Napoleonic Wars, French caricatures satirized English soldiers occupying Paris as "Petits'maîtres." In these prints the English occupation was ridiculed by portraying the English soldiers as bullies or fops.   A.J.

GEORGE CRUIKSHANK
British, 1792-1878

52 *The Fox & The Goose; or, Boney Broke Loose!*   March 17, 1815
     (see p. 30)
BM 12506
Broadley, I, 369; app. 312, no. 354
Cohn 1126
Coll. de Vinck 9519
Hand-coloured etching
28.0 x 40.7 cm (imp.)
Gift of Dr. and Mrs. Gilbert Bagnani, 1981
Acc. no. 81/270

Having escaped from the fortified isle of Elba, Napoleon landed on the southern coast of France on March 1, 1815, with 1,500 soldiers (*Historical Dictionary of France from the Restoration,* 1141). The news reached London on March 10 and the first caricature to reflect it was Cruikshank's *The Fox & The Goose; or, Boney Broke Loose!*, which appeared on March 17. Cruikshank's caricature is based on the drawing of an amateur and resembles a child's illustration (George, *English Caricature 1793-1832*, 160).

A tiny mounted man, probably the British commissioner in Elba, calls out "Stole away!!! Stole away!!!" while Napoleon, in the guise of a fox, runs across France to Paris, accompanied by the bees that were emblematic of the Bonapartists. Everywhere people flee to the coast while the Bourbon cavalry and infantry stand ready to defend the country. Geese carry the news of Napoleon's escape to the Congress of Vienna, which is symbolized by the box in the top left corner. The representatives of the countries at the Congress of Vienna are satirized as birds who sit around a table in a room resembling an alehouse. Recognizable from left to right are the Tsar of Russia, the King of Prussia, and the Emperor of Austria. Sitting in front of the table is the Duke of Wellington (BM 12506; Coll. de Vinck 9519). Cruikshank's caricature blames Napoleon's successful escape on the political bickering at the Congress of Vienna (George, *English Caricature 1793-1832*, 160).   A.J.

Attributed to THOMAS ROWLANDSON
British, 1756-1827

53 *Vive Le Roi! Vive L'Empereur. Vive Le Diable*   April/May 1815
     (see p. 29)
BM 12531
Broadley, I, 383; app. 341, no. 866
Grego, II, 291
Hand-coloured etching
30.1 x 22.2 cm (imp.)
Gift of J. T. Johnson, 1981
Acc. no. 81/235

The ease with which the French seemed able to welcome Napoleon one month and the Bourbon king the next drew vicious criticism from across the Channel. In 1815 there were many English caricatures that ridiculed the vacillating political loyalties of the French (Duffy, 352).

In this caricature, Rowlandson presents a fearsome French soldier whose bearing is full of contradictions. His cocked hat bears signs declaring three allegiances: to the Emperor, to the King, and to the Devil. His uniform is neat and smart while his feet are bare, and in his right arm he carries a musket, while in the other he holds a snuff box. In the background are more symbols of French fickleness: the windmill which is ironically titled

"French Stability" and the cat and ape embracing which refers to the National Guard and the soldiers who cheered Napoleon's return (BM 12531).   A.J.

ANONYMOUS
French, early 19th century

54 *La Bonne Charge!!*   April 8, 1815
BF 17: (April 29, 1815), 194, no. 355
Broadley, app. 366, no. 144
Coll. de Vinck 9442
Hand-coloured etching and stipple on laid paper
25.6 x 33.0 cm (imp.)
Gift of the Trier-Fodor Foundation, 1986
Acc. no. 85/472

Satires during Napoleon's One Hundred Days, from April to June 1815 were severely critical of Louis XVIII. Caricatures ridiculed the inept and greedy Bourbon monarchy and exploited the theme of Louis XVIII's speedy flight to escape from Napoleon on March 19, 1815, as a means of mocking the king's lack of courage (Broadley, *Napoleon*, II, 61).

In this satire, Louis XVIII is shown fleeing with the comte d'Artois, duc d'Angoulême, and duc de Berry while a bust of Napoleon glows on the horizon. Louis XVIII steals away with the royal jewels, which had recently been evaluated and were considered a fortune "extraordinaire" (Coll. de Vinck 9442).

On the heads of the king's aides are snuffers, which were symbols used in French satire to attack a repressive government. The image of the snuffer ("éteignoir") harks back to the time of Louis XV when it was used to mock the king's attempts to extinguish the intellectual flame kindled by Voltaire, Rousseau, and the *philosophes*. During the Restoration, the motif of the snuffer was frequently employed to attack the conservative policies of Louis XVIII and Charles X (Broadley, *Napoleon*, II, 97-98).   A.J.

ANONYMOUS
French, early 19th century

55 *Le départ des quatre fils Aymon*   April 13, 1815
BF 16: (April 22, 1815), 183, no. 326
Coll. de Vinck 9455
Hand-coloured etching on wove paper
23.5 x 29.0 cm (imp.)
Gift of the Trier-Fodor Foundation, 1986
Acc. no. 85/475

This caricature was inspired by the sudden flight of the Bourbons. Four royalists representing the Household Cavalry, the King's

54 Anonymous (French), *La Bonne Charge!!*, April 8, 1815

55 Anonymous (French), *Le départ des quatre fils Amyon*, April 13, 1815

Soldiers, the Black Musketeers and the King's Guardsmen flee. Their impressive uniforms are belittled by their ignoble facial expressions and scrawny horse (Coll. de Vinck 9455).

The title refers to the medieval tale of Renaud and his three brothers, sons of Aymon of Dordogne, who escape from the emperor's court on their magical horse Bayard after Renaud kills one of Charlemagne's nephews in a fray (*Oxford Companion to French Literature*).   A.J.

LE DÉPART DU DIRECTEUR DE PROVINCE.

Déposé à la Bib.ᵗ Imp.ᵗᵉ

56 Anonymous (French), *Le Départ du Directeur de Province,* c.1815

ANONYMOUS
French, early 19th century

56 *Le Départ du Directeur de Province*   c.1815
Hand-coloured etching and stipple on laid paper
22.5 x 32.0 cm (sheet)
Gift of the Trier-Fodor Foundation, 1986
Acc. no. 85/470

Originally executed in 1804, then reprinted in 1815 and 1816, *Le Départ du Directeur de Province*, like the majority of the carica-tures at this time, indirectly ridicules the flights of Napoleon in 1814 and 1815 and of Louis XVIII in 1815 (Simond, 361).

In this caricature the Director leaves in a carriage with his companion and various pets. In the hand of the Director is a play titled *Impromptu Voyage, A New Work in Two Acts*. Behind the carriage actors in the exotic costumes of Voltaire's famous play *Zaïre* clamour after the departing Director, while pieces of paper titled "Ticket of Administration, good anywhere, for the entire year" fall from an open trunk. Above the door of the theatre is the announcement for *Zaïre* and also for the second play, *The Unex-pected Return*.   A. J.

57 Anonymous (French), *Charge Contre Napoleon I* or *le père la violette, chiffonier ou des placets comme s'il en pleuvait,* September 4, 1815

ANONYMOUS
French, early 19th century

57 *Charge Contre Napoleon I* or *le père la violette, chiffonnier ou des placets comme s'il en pleuvait*   September 4, 1815
BF 37: (September 16, 1815), 391, no. 855
Broadley, II, 71; app. 375, no. 277
Hand-coloured etching on laid paper
23.1 x 29.8 cm (imp.)
Gift of the Trier-Fodor Foundation, 1982
Acc. no. 82/239

This is one of a pair of anti-Napoleonic caricatures that satirize the returning leader as a "rag picker." In the caricature not shown here, entitled *"la Violette, the Scavenger,"* Napoleon is shown searching for his crown in a heap of garbage. In *le père la violette, chifonnier ou des placets comme s'il en pleuvait* (Father Violet as ragman, or it rains petitions) Napoleon crosses the street of the "Tiger without his Crown" followed by either Grand Marshal of the Palace General Henri Gratien Bertrand (1773-1844) or Michel Ney (1769-1815), marshal of France. Napoleon gathers the many petitions that the poor thrust towards him. One reads: "I was paid to cry 'Vive l'Empereur' for three days and have only been paid five francs, ten more are owing me." From the window a woman bemoans the loss of life during the wars: "I have given twenty-five children to Napoleon, I wish to keep the twenty-sixth so as not to let my race die out" (Broadley, *Napoleon,* II, 70-71; Clerc, 210). Indeed the burden of the Napoleonic Wars fell heavily on the peasantry who, unlike the wealthier classes, could not afford to buy a substitute to fight for them (*Historical Diction-ary of Napoleonic France*, 126-127).

The reference to violets in the title of this caricature corresponds to the declaration Napoleon made upon leaving for the island of Elba, that he would return in the violet season. Violets became a secret rallying cry for Napoleon's supporters; they wore violets in their hats and lapels, referred to them in conversation and incorporated the image into prints to communicate their loyalties (Broadley, *Napoleon*, II, 93).   A.J.

ANONYMOUS
French, early 19th century

58 *Le Lutrin de Boileau*   August 31, 1815
Coll. de Vinck 10280
Hand-coloured etching on laid paper
33.8 x 24.2 cm (imp.)
Gift of the Trier-Fodor Foundation, 1982
Acc. no. 82/238

Nicolas Boileau-Despréaux (1636-1711) was a famous literary figure of the seventeenth century who enjoyed success during his lifetime: he was Louis XIV's historiographer; he became a member of the Académie Française; and among his colleagues were Molière, Racine, and La Fontaine. Although it has been claimed that Boileau founded the tradition of French literary criticism, he is largely remembered for his mock-heroic poems (*Oxford Companion to French Literature*).

Between 1674 and 1683, Boileau published his famous mock-heroic poem *Le Lutrin*. The idea for this caricature was sparked by the story of a dispute over the positioning of the lectern in Sainte-Chapelle in Paris. That the print refers to Boileau's critical piece about the Church is indicative of the anti-clerical sentiment prevalent in France in 1815.

Boileau's poem tells of a lectern that was mysteriously overturned one night. The dean suspects the precentor (who leads the congregation in singing), since the lectern cast a shadow on his seat in the choir. Fearing that his leadership is threatened, the dean turns to his flock for help. Names are drawn and three brave souls are sent to resurrect the lectern.

With the aid of wine to foster courage, Boirude the Sexton, Bointrin, and John the clock-maker, set out at night on their mission. In the process of replacing the lectern, they disturb an owl that had been nesting inside the podium.

Out flies the broad-fac'd Chorister of the Night,
And with her russling wings strikes out the Light:
This struck their Souls with horrible Confusion,
Amaz'd they stand, they doubt; but in conclusion,

58 Anonymous (French), *Le Lutrin de Boileau*, August 31, 1815

As soon as Fear lent them use of Feet
Away they trudge, fill'd with shame and Regret;
The Nave they soon recover; whil'st their hair
Stands bristling on their heads, dissolving fear
Makes their Knees quiver underneath their Bodies
(Boileau, 26).

Found hiding on the porch, the "three great Champions" are upbraided for their cowardice. They return to seek revenge on the owl which has already flown away.

The dispute continues but in the end the dean emerges victorious, and the defeated precentor sulks in his seat hidden from view by the restored lectern.   A.J.

59 Sébastien Coeuré, *Le Sermon de Village,* May 19, 1815

60 Anonymous (French), *A Bas la Calotte!!!* from *Les Amusemens du Peuple,* June 5, 1815

SEBASTIEN COEURE
French, b. 1788, fl. 1810-1831

59 *Le Sermon de Village* May 19, 1815
BF 21: (May 27, 1815), 246, no. 512
Coll. de Vinck 10273
Inventaire 19 s., v, 64, no. 4
Hand-coloured etching and stipple on laid paper
24.0 x 32.9 cm (imp.)
Gift of the Trier-Fodor Foundation, 1986
Acc. no. 85/507

The early nineteenth century witnessed a fervent religious revival, but while the number of clergy escalated, so too did the disdain and hatred for the Church by the educated classes. When this caricature was published in 1815, the antagonism between clergy and anti-clerical forces had reached fever pitch (Cobban, II, 74, 82-83). While Coeuré's satire ridicules the *naïveté* of the peasants, it viciously attacks the despotism of the clergy. A.J.

ANONYMOUS
French, early 19th century

60 *A Bas la Calotte!!!* from *Les Amusemens du Peuple* June 5, 1815
BF 27: (July 8, 1815), 303, no. 617
Coll. de Vinck 8721
Hand-coloured etching and stipple engraving on laid paper
21.7 x 29.7 cm (imp.)
Gift of the Trier-Fodor Foundation, 1986
Acc. no. 85/506

This caricature deals with the issue of religious toleration guaranteed in the Charter of 1814. Louis XVIII had promised equality and liberty before the law, regardless of religious affiliation (Cobban,

II, 74). In January 1815, the king was put to the test.

In 1802, Abbé Marduel, the priest of Saint Roch in Paris, refused to bury Mademoiselle Chameroy, a dancer, whom he considered excommunicated because of her profession. The priest was severely chastised for this and sent on a three-month retreat (Coll. de Vinck 8690). In 1815 he once again refused to bury the body of the well-known actress Mademoiselle Raucourt (Coll. de Vinck 8721). On the day of her funeral, a sizeable crowd, including the famous French actor Talma, gathered to pay their last respects. When the priest refused to perform the service, the crowd marched on the Tuileries Palace, where Louis XVIII, in order to put an end to the demonstration, pronounced that anyone who had been baptised had the right to be buried (Simond, 319-321). The king thus upheld the law of the Charter over the law of the Church.

This sheet shows a group of peasants violently opposed to the recently sanctioned burial of Mademoiselle Raucourt. While the Abbé Marduel cowers behind the window, the angry peasants try to grab the priest's skull cap, known as a "calotte," from the stick extended from the church. A hussar, representative of the king's authority, violently enforces the royal declaration by threatening the peasants. On the wall are two signs: one announcing the funeral service for Mademoiselle Raucourt, the other foreshadowing a violent end for the priest at the hands of the peasants if he permits the burial. The sign proclaims that he will end up at the Church of the "Quinze Vingts," a hospital in Paris for the blind, deaf, and poor (Hillairet, I, 425-426).

A Bas la Calotte!!! (Down with the priest) was published several months after the event during Napoleon's One Hundred Days. The violets in the peasant's apron are symbolic of Napoleon's expected return. (See *Charge Contre Napoleon* I, cat. no. 57, for the significance of violets). A.J.

ANONYMOUS
French, early 19th century

61 *Progrès des Lumières* c.1820 (see p. 7)
Hand-coloured etching on wove paper
26.8 x 40.3 cm (imp.)
Gift of the Trier-Fodor Foundation, 1986
Acc. no. 85/476

Progrès des Lumières is a satire against the Christian Brothers, a society of religious laymen devoted to elementary education. They were suppressed in 1792 by the Revolutionary government, but were reinstated by Napoleon in 1803. They grew in popularity during the religious revival of the Restoration, and increased their schools from four in 1811 to 320 in 1830 (*Historical Dictionary of France from the Restoration*, 133).

In this caricature, the Christian Brothers try to pull down the sign of the "Enseignment Mutuel." The Ecole Mutuelle was a new method of education that had been introduced to France in the early nineteenth century in order to teach larger groups of students more quickly and cheaply. The system had been founded in England by a Quaker named John Lancaster and was based on the principle of shared learning: older boys taught the younger ones under the guidance of a supervisor (*Historical Dictionary of France from the Restoration*, 855 and 373).

There was a great deal of antagonism between the two schools; the Ecole Mutuel was Protestant and represented the modern approach to teaching, whereas the Christian Brothers were staunchly Catholic and adhered to the traditional method of strict discipline (Marlet, 46). In this satire the Christian Brothers are portrayed as the bastions of conservatism as they try to destroy the more progressive school.

There are a number of symbols in this satire of the reactionary behaviour of the Christian Brothers. The crayfish on the right was associated with the reactionary policies of Louis XVIII and Charles X. Its impregnable shell and slow backward motion made it an appropriate metaphor for conservatism (Grand-Carteret, 185). The Christian Brothers are aided by a royalist, the gentleman in the wig and court dress. The inscription "Journal des Débats" on the wall to the left refers to an ultra-royalist Paris journal (*Oxford Companion to French Literature*).

Even more scathing is the reference to "Lumières" in the title of this satire. "Lumières" was the great philosophical movement of the eighteenth century that advocated progress and reason above tradition and religion, giving us the English term Enlightenment (*Petit Larousse*). The Christian Brothers are portrayed as making a mockery of the ideas that had sparked the Revolution in 1789. A.J.

62 Anonymous (French), *Aye qu'il fait froid* from *Le Suprême Bon Ton, No. 20*, February 1816

ANONYMOUS
French, early 19th century

62 *Aye qu'il fait froid* from *Le Suprême Bon Ton, No. 20*
February 1816
BF 7: (February 17, 1816), 71, no. 120
Hand-coloured etching and stipple on wove paper
18.5 x 26.0 cm (image)
Gift of the Trier-Fodor Foundation, 1986
Acc. no. 85/474

Aye qu'il fait froid (Oh, it's cold!) portrays a bourgeois gentleman in his nightcap, shivering by the fire. This print offers a view of the interior of a fashionable home during the Restoration.

The clothing of the lady crouched before the fire shows the influence of Tudor fashion during the late Empire. At the time dresses "à la Marie Stuart" were the rage (Laver, *Taste and Fashion*, 27). These dresses had puffed sleeves, high necklines, and ruffed collars known as "Betsies," a name derived from their originator, Queen Elizabeth I (*Historical Dictionary of Napoleonic France*, 118).

The neoclassical apartments of the early nineteenth century were anything but luxurious. The elegant Empire furniture starkly contrasts with the filth and chaos that prevailed in many fashionable apartments. English accounts tell of dirty stairwells and the awkward layout of rooms: there was no dining room; the kitchen was located outside the building; and the bathroom, if there was one, was just a tiny cubby-hole with a basin of water. The wood-burning fires used to heat the homes were inefficient. It took until noon to heat the rooms, and the dirt and soot contributed to the general state of disorder (Robiquet, 82-89). A.J.

Réunion Gastronomique
OU LES GOURMANDS A TABLE

63 Anonymous (French), *Réunion Gastronomique ou Les Gourmands à Table*, c.1820

ANONYMOUS
French, early 19th century

63 *Réunion Gastronomique ou Les Gourmands à Table*   c.1820
Hand-coloured etching on wove paper
24.1 x 33.3 cm (sheet)
Gift of the Trier-Fodor Foundation, 1986
Acc. no. 85/477

Gluttony was a popular theme in the graphic satire of the Empire and Restoration (Grand-Carteret, 79) and was an excellent vehicle for debasing the newly self-important bourgeoisie. This anonymous work is remarkably similar to Rowlandson's etching, *This World is a well furnished Table* (fig. 13). In these two prints a group of men sit around a long table gorging themselves; the animalistic tone is heightened by the presence of the English bull dogs of the type imported to France during periods of anglomania (Laver, *Taste and Fashion*, 16). The figure in the foreground, with

his belly bulging, is reminiscent of Gillray's work, *A Voluptuary under the horrors of Digestion* (fig. 14). These references to English satire leave no doubt that the French caricaturists were aware of, if not fairly well versed in, English caricature (Grand-Carteret, 92).

In the right corner of *Réunion Gastronomique ou Les Gourmands à Table* is an open book titled *Almanach des Gourmands*, which refers to a popular recipe book published in eight volumes between 1803 and 1812. The author, Grimod de la Reynière, is said to have "put poetry into his sauces, wit into his condiments." He founded a twelve-member academy that met each week to try new dishes and to bestow Certificates of Official Recognition on the ones that titillated their palates. This scene may allude to their weekly rendezvous (Robiquet, 94).

Eating out became popular in the nineteenth century as the French took up the English custom of eating in restaurants (Laver, *Taste and Fashion*, 16). In Paris, at a respectable restaur-

fig. 13

Thomas Rowlandson, *This World is a well furnished Table,* 1811; coloured etching, 23.8 x 35.6 cm. Art Gallery of Ontario, gift of Mrs. M. Lyle, 1942, Acc. no. 2701.

ant, a meal including four to five main dishes, wine or champagne, dessert, coffee, and a liqueur could be bought for under ten francs. In some restaurants, one would be faced with a choice of thirteen soups, twenty-two hors-d'oeuvres, one-hundred-and-nine meat and fish dishes, thirty-nine desserts, fifty-two wines, and twelve liqueurs (Blagdon, I, 443-456)!

This caricature is dedicated to the gluttons "de Paris et des Départements" and must therefore also be seen as an attack on the politicians representing the City of Paris and the ninety-five administrative departments of France.   A. J.

fig. 14   James Gillray, *A Voluptuary under the horrors of Digestion,* July 1792; Wright 85, BM 8112, etching on wove paper, 36.5 x 29.5 cm. Art Gallery of Ontario, gift of the Trier-Fodor Foundation, 1985, Acc. no. 85/41.

LE BOULEVARD DE GAND A PARIS.
Le Suprême Bon-Ton N.º 27.

à Paris chez Martinet.   2 fr.   Déposé 18.ª

64 Adrien-Pierre-François Godefroy, *Le Boulevard de Gand a Paris* from *Le Suprême Bon Ton No. 27*, September 1816

ADRIEN-PIERRE-FRANÇOIS GODEFROY
French, 1777-1865

64 *Le Boulevard de Gand a Paris* from *Le Suprême Bon-Ton No. 27*
      September 1816
   BF 38: (September 21, 1816), 415, no. 816
   Inventaire 19 s., IX, 208, no. 24
   Hand-coloured etching on wove paper
   23.6 x 32.1 cm (sheet)
   Gift of the Trier-Fodor Foundation, 1986
   Acc. no. 85/518

Fashionable Parisians and English tourists flocked to the boulevards in Paris. Along these wide roads one could find every sort of public entertainment: musicians, exhibitions, temples, ballrooms, hotels, coffee houses, restaurants – indeed, "everything that ingenuity can imagine for the diversion of the idle stroller," exclaimed one English visitor (Blagdon, I, 305).

The Boulevard de Gand was originally created for military purposes in 1685. By Napoleon's time, it had become a wide road of beaten earth with two rows of elm trees. Barriers were constructed during the Empire to protect pedestrians from traffic. It earned its name during the Restoration from the town where Louis XVIII fled during Napoleon's One Hundred Days. Later the Boulevard was named after the popular Théâtre des Italiens (Hillairet, I, 661-662; *Grand Dictionnaire Universal*, VIII, 980; Robiquet, 132).

This is another work that reveals the anglomania that came with improved diplomatic relations in 1814. Among the many imports from England were horses and carriages, English cloth, and English tailors. Here two gentlemen exhibit the fashions of English dandies that were popular with French gentlemen (Laver, *Taste and Fashion*, 16, 24). The figure on the right wears large baggy pants called "Cossacks," which had become the rage in London in 1813 when two Russian officers appeared there in full dress (Duffy, 344).   A. J.

ADRIEN-PIERRE-FRANÇOIS GODEFROY
French, 1777-1865

65 *La Course des Montagnes Russes à Paris* from *Le Suprême Bon-Ton,*
   N°. 29 November 1816 (see p. 33)
   BF 44: (November 2, 1816), 486, no. 883
   Inventaire 19 s., IX, 208, no. 24
   Hand-coloured etching and stipple on wove paper
   25.7 x 34.4 cm (imp.)
   Gift of the Trier-Fodor Foundation, 1986
   Acc. no. 85/519

Restoration society, having reaped the benefits of an economic boom in the first decade of the nineteenth century, was excessively materialistic (*Historical Dictionary of France from the Restoration,* 379-383). A new generation had emerged oblivious of the patriotic fervour of 1789, and for whom money was the new cult (Simond, 306). Like the caricatures of the Empire, those of the Restoration focused primarily on the "*moeurs,*" the fashions and manners of this opulent society. All the latest crazes provided rich sources for caricature, including marriage agencies, velocipedes, kaleidoscopes, and skating (Grand Carteret, 119).

The fad for roller-coasters appears in many caricatures from 1816 to 1823: The "Montagnes russes" (Russian mountains), the first slide to be erected, enjoyed a monopoly until the rage became so great that construction began on more slides all over the city. Within a short time Paris could boast of six slides. These were essentially high towers from which wooden seats on rollers descended steep ramps. One slide incorporated a restaurant and a café, and an immense mirror at the highest point of the ramp that could be seen at night from various parts of the city (Scribe, III, 4, 21, 27; Simond, 379-380).

Accidents were frequent; but despite the many broken bones – and noses – Parisians remained undaunted and continued to patronize the slides. Not surprisingly, a term was coined to describe this insane fever: "casse-têtomanie." The excessive danger posed by the slides eventually forced the authorities to intervene and close them (Grand-Carteret, 120). A.J.

ANONYMOUS
French, early 19th century

66 *Monsieur Calicot partant pour le Combat des Montagnes*
   August 1817 (see colour plate on p. 45)
   BF 33: (August 16, 1817), 463, no. 649
   Lithograph on wove paper
   33.2 x 22.2 cm (sheet)
   Gift of the Trier-Fodor Foundation, 1982
   Acc. no. 82/237

Eugène Scribe (1791-1861) was one of the most prolific and successful playwrights of the early nineteenth century. He wrote over three hundred plays, most of which satirized bourgeois life. In *Combat des Montagnes* (a whimsical piece, poking fun at the roller-coasters in Paris), Scribe created the character M. Calicot, a seller of novelties, who liked to parade as a war veteran wearing spurs, moustache, and a red carnation. His vanity made a mockery of the sacred memory of the brave men who had fought and died in the Napoleonic Wars (Scribe, III, 4-5).

The word "calicot" refers to the cotton industry, which had undergone a small revolution during the Empire and was at that time one of France's strongest industries. This industry's prosperity reflected the growing demand of the middle class for cotton goods to satisfy their fashion needs (*Historical Dictionary of France from the Restoration,* 379-381; *Historical Dictionary of Napoleonic France,* 162-163). "Calicot" also has the derogatory meaning of a "counter jumper" – a scheming businessman. The character of M. Calicot was similar to a dandy in attitude and attire; he was vain, selfish, and opportunistic.

The drapers (sellers of cloth) in Paris interpreted Scribe's play as a forthright criticism of their profession. Angered, they swore to stop further productions and to remove the actor playing M. Calicot. For several nights they besieged the theatre, drawing a great deal of public attention. The police, by arresting some of the drapers, halted these riots. The behaviour of the drapers only reinforced Scribe's accusations of shallow self-interest (Simond, 380-382).

Following the production of Scribe's play in July 1817, a flood of caricatures titled "War of the Calicots" appeared. In them the drapers are represented by M. Calicot, portrayed as a dandified cloth merchant with spurs, moustache, and red carnation. The figure of the "Calicot" was used frequently during the Restoration, and constituted a bitter attack on the bourgeoisie (Grand-Carteret, 121-124). In *Monsieur Calicot partant pour le Combat des Montagnes,* the story of Scribe's play and the drapers have become intertwined; a dapper "Calicot" figure leaves for the theatre; instead of regular army equipment he carries the tools of the draper's trade. A.J.

fig. 15 Jacques-Louis David, *Oath of the Horatii*, 1784; oil on canvas, 33.0 x 42.5 cm.
By permission of the Musée du Louvre, Paris.

ANONYMOUS
French, early 19th century

67 *Serment des Calicots* c.August 1817 (see cover)
Hand-coloured lithograph on wove paper
27.7 x 39.7 cm (sheet)
Gift of the Trier-Fodor Foundation, 1982
Acc. no. 82/240

Another satire that deals with the theme of the Calicots is *Serment des Calicots*. Its humour lies in equating the prosaic intentions of the Calicots with the devotion of the soldiers in *Oath of the Horatii* (1784) (fig. 15) by Jacques-Louis David (1748-1825), in which three brothers swear in front of their father to fight to the death for Rome. The pledge is made to yardsticks rather than to swords; Roman arches and columns have disappeared, and the "mourners" on the left are tearful and bored.

The *Oath of the Horatii* was known throughout France as one of the first works of art to exalt the idea of sacrifice for one's native land. It personified Roman virtue and patriotism, which were seen as the basis of the ideals of the French Revolution (Friedlaender, 14-17). *Serment des Calicots* on the other hand praises the ideals of the Restoration society: materialism and self-gain. This satire reduced the sublime message of the painting to one of base, human greed.

This is not the only time David's famous painting was used by caricaturists. Another satire, *Serment des Voraces*, portrays three men with gaping mouths swearing to three forks and a bottle of wine (Bornemann, 129).

Serment des Calicots is one of the earliest examples of a new process of printing, lithography, which was invented in 1798 by Alois Senefelder in Munich, and introduced into France in 1802.

Lithography revolutionized caricature during the 1830s, as this durable printing process made possible the printing of much larger editions for the use of newspapers and journals, which was not possible as long as caricature was confined to the much softer, etched copper plate. A. J.

ANONYMOUS
French, late 18th century

68 *Prenez Y Garde!!!* September 1817
BF 38: (September 20, 1817), 529, no. 782
Hand-coloured lithograph on wove paper
28.3 x 35.0 cm (sheet)
Gift of the Trier-Fodor Foundation, 1982
Acc. no. 82/253

This caricature was designed to warn the Restoration audience against three types of capitalists who prospered during this period of economic boom. From left to right are the seller of rare and expensive French cashmere; the Calicot, merchant of novelties; and the gawky English salesman who was bringing foreign products to France. A. J.

69 Anonymous (French), *Quelques Singes de France*, December 1817

92

PRENEZ Y GARDE !!!

Il existe une trés grande différence entre .

* Le Casimir Français.   Le Calicot de Paris.   et le vrai Pekin Anglais !

Le 1.er est bon teint, devenu rare parcequ'on l'a prodigué, mais il est très estimé et toujours d'une rare valeur !!!

Celui-ci est mauvais teint, aussi blanchit-il facilement, on le trouve dans les magasins de nouveautés à très bas prix, malgré la hausse qui en a été faite ...

Impayable ! parcequ'il est original ! Nous sommes inondés de cette marchandise ...

68 Anonymous (French), *Prenez Y Garde!!!*, September 1817

ANONYMOUS
French, late 18th century

69 *Quelques Singes de France*   December 1817
   BF 51: (December 20, 1817), 700, no. 1123
   Hand-coloured etching on laid paper
   30.6 x 21.6 cm (imp.)
   Gift of the Trier-Fodor Foundation, 1982
   Acc. no. 82/251

In the centre is a domed building, the Institut de France; located beside the Seine on the Quai de Conti, it has housed the five French academies since 1805. They were famous for their exclusivity: entrance was granted only to those who were elected and had their appointment approved by the head of state (*Oxford Companion to French Literature*). The boarded-up walls and windows probably symbolize the impregnability of the academies, and the hopelessness of gaining entrance. The two mischievous men on the sidewalk appear to be soliciting votes from an innocent bystander.   A.J.

Pl: XVIII

A FRENCH ELEPHANT.

70 Anonymous (British), *A French Elephant*, c.November 1818

ANONYMOUS
British, early 19th century

70 *A French Elephant*   c.November 1818
BM 13008B
Coll. de Vinck 9102, English reprint of Hennin 13871
Hand-coloured etching on laid paper
32.1 x 22.7 cm (imp.)
Gift of the Trier-Fodor Foundation, 1981
Acc. no. 81/186

This etching was made after a lithograph by George Cruikshank in 1818. Cruikshank borrowed the idea from a French crayon drawing entitled *Eléphant vu par derrière* of May 1814 (Coll. de Vinck 9102; BM 13008).

In this caricature, the obese King Louis XVIII, who was elevated to the throne of France in May 1814 at the age of 59, is metamorphosed into an elephant. The king's shoulders have become the elephant's hindquarters, and his wisps of grey hair the ears. A long, thin coat-tail hangs like an elephant's tail between a pair of thick legs, which no doubt allude to the fact that Louis XVIII

suffered from gout and walked with great difficulty (Cobban, II, 71). Across the king's back is a ribbon from which hangs the French fleur-de-lis.

This caricature is a superb example of personal satire. The prominent physical attributes of the king, his age, weight, and gout, have been ludicrously exaggerated (Streicher, 431-437; Geipel, 22-26). This satire foreshadows the work of Charles Philipon in the 1830s in which the rotund King Louis Philippe is reduced to a pear (Maurice, 70-71, with reproduction).   A.J.

GEORGE CRUIKSHANK
British, 1792-1878

71 *Traveling in France – or, – Le depart dela diligence*   October 19, 1818 (see colour plate on p. 46)
BM 13053
Cohn 2043
Hand-coloured etching on wove paper
25.4 x 35.4 cm (imp.)
Gift of the Trier-Fodor Foundation, 1980
Acc. no. 80/39

Gillray's death in 1815 marks the end of the "golden age" of caricature in England. *Traveling in France* is typical of the gentle social satire that in the 1820s replaced the bitter political caricature. The nation was tired of war and politics, and conservative Regency society found the savagery and vulgarity of Gillray's pen intolerable. Thus Cruikshank, who had commenced his career in the same vein as Gillray, devoted himself to social satire in the 1820s and to book illustration in the 1830s (Geipel, 73; Brown University, 11).

Traveling in France, which pokes fun at English tourists in France, undoubtedly was influenced by William Hogarth's *The*

fig. 16   William Hogarth, *The Stage Coach, or Country Inn Yard,* June 1747; BM 2882, etching and engraving, 20.7 x 30.3 cm. Reproduced by permission of the Trustees of the British Museum.

94

Stage Coach of 1747 (fig. 16). In Cruikshank's print a large coach prepares to transport English tourists to Paris: while two dandies help a fashionable lady to board, a snooty John Bull, probably her husband, pulls money from his pocket to pay the innkeeper. One English eyewitness reported that invalids and beggars were a common sight at the post houses (Scott, 34). The little dog is typical of the dogs shaved in the French manner that were sold to tourists at Calais (BM, 13053).

For English travellers the voyage to France was full of obstacles. After purchasing passage on a ship, one had to wait for the wind and tide before crossing the Channel. Depending on weather conditions, the trip from Dover to Calais could take as little as three hours or as long as two days. If the tide was out when they arrived in France the passengers faced up to a three-mile walk across mud flats. If the boat arrived late in the evening, visitors were forced to spend the night outside the closed gates of Calais (Maxwell, 19-22).

The next stage in the journey was by "diligence," a large coach seating twenty to thirty passengers, with a conductor and driver. While it was usually crowded and uncomfortable it was cheap and prompt, and could, if necessary, travel up to seventy miles a day (Maxwell, 22-23). During the Revolution, the roads to Paris were dangerous and fell into a state of disrepair, but by 1815 they were in excellent condition (Maxwell, 27). Under ideal conditions, Paris could be reached from Calais in thirty-six hours (Blagdon, I, 11). There were frequent delays because of accidents like flooding, forced detours, axles catching on fire, robberies, and intoxicated drivers (Maxwell, 27).

Along the route to Paris the traveller also had to contend with eager hotel owners who often overcharged their patrons. In some cases, the presentation of the bill led to violence (Maxwell, 31).   A.J.

ISAAC ROBERT CRUIKSHANK
English, 1789-1856

72 *Exquisite Dandies*   1818
Hand-coloured etching on wove paper
35.6 x 25.0 cm (sheet)
Gift of the Trier-Fodor Foundation, 1982
Acc. no. 81/167

In *Exquisite Dandies*, Isaac Robert Cruikshank (1789-1856) a brother to the famous George Cruikshank, paints a vulgar picture of the excessive vanities of the English dandies.

The style of the dandies originated with George Bryan "Beau" Brummell who was the most fashionable gentleman of George III's court. Brummell was synonymous with elegance; he wore sombre-coloured suits that were expertly tailored from the finest cloths and elaborate ties that were always immaculate after he

72 Isaac Robert Cruikshank, *Exquisite Dandies*, 1818

had spent a great deal of time in front of the mirror. Brummel had to flee the country in 1816 to escape his creditors, and in the wake of his departure his ideas were taken *ad absurdum* by fashionable young men. The "dandies," as his followers were called, wore top hats that swelled at the top, high starched collars (that sometimes came up over their eyes), outrageously extravagant neck ties, skin-tight breeches, and chicken-skin gloves. Their effeminate tendencies extended to the application of rouge to their faces, and pads and corsets to imitate the female hour-glass shape. They also inherited from Brummell a concern for personal hygiene; they were clean shaven, wore fresh linen, brushed their teeth, and took frequent baths (Laver, *Concise History of Costume*, 158-162; Angeloglou, 88-92; Cunnington, *Nineteenth, Century* 77-87; George, *Hogarth to Cruikshank*, 164).

From 1818 to 1819, dandies were featured in English caricature. They were seen as symbols of a revolt against the bourgeois ethic of work and frugality. They were insolent, arrogant, effeminate fops who resembled the English Macaronis of the early 1770s (George, *Hogarth to Cruikshank*, 163-166).   A.J.

Toujours des farces.

quelle indignité.

74 Anonymous (French), *Toujours des farces,* January 1820

ANONYMOUS
French, early 19th century

73 *Lord-gueil Lady-scorde*   April 27, 1819 (see p. x)
(see p. x)
Coll. de Vinck 9293
Hand-coloured etching on laid paper
35.1 x 24.7 cm (imp.)
Gift of the Trier-Fodor Foundation, 1982
Acc. no. 82/256

This caricature belongs to a series entitled *Caricature Anglaise.* This print, however, differs slightly from the rest of the caricatures in the series because the series title in the top margin has been replaced by "Les Passions." Also, part of the inscription in the lower margin has been scratched out. The full inscription should read "Lord-gueil s'unit à Lady-scorde" (Pride units with Discord) (Coll. de Vinck 9293), a brilliant play on words since "Lord-gueil" and "Lady-scorde" are puns on the French "*l'orgueil*" and "*la discorde*."

Pride, represented as an obese English officer, aggressively grabs the hand of Discord who looks like one of the Furies, and tries to blow out the flame of her torch. They stand on a pier while a battle rages in the background. One source proposes that the intention of this caricature was to provoke war (Coll. de Vinck 9293). It is most likely a reference to the tumultuous political situation in England. With the advance of the Reform Movement, there were increasing incidents of violence such as the Peterloo Massacre that occurred in August 1819 (George, *English Political Caricature 1793-1832*, 180-181).   A.J.

ANONYMOUS
French, early 19th century
Lithograph by CHARLES MOTTE
French, 1785-1836

74 *Toujours des farces*   January 1820
Coll. de Vinck 8748-8755
BF 2: (January 8, 1820), 22, no. 16
Hand-coloured lithograph on wove paper
25.8 x 30.1 cm (sight, sheet)
Gift of the Trier-Fodor Foundation, 1986
Acc. no. 85/480

At the end of 1819, newspapers printed stories of a maniac running loose in the city who poked women with his sword. Parisians were perversely enthralled. The subject dominated conversation, and details of the attacks and injuries to the victims became the focus of sordid interest. Intrigue quickly led to panic. Women began to imagine themselves victims and everywhere ran from men approaching too quickly on the street. To quell this hysteria, the police conducted an investigation in December that revealed that the number of the attacks had been exaggerated.

The press had the last word: from December 13 to 24 a series of caricatures appeared portraying the "poker" and the "poked." *Toujours des farces*, most likely part of this series, shows a well-dressed lady accosted on the street by an officer. Her reaction, "What an indignity," hardly seems one of distress, rather one of perverse delight.   A. J.

AUGUSTE BOUQUET
French, 1810-1846

75 *Mr. Thiers* from *La Caricature*, no. 144   August 8, 1833
Inventaire 19 s., III, 246, no. 12
Hand-coloured lithograph on light yellow paper
35.3 x 26.7 cm (sheet)
Gift of the Trier-Fodor Foundation, 1981
Acc. no. 81/44

Auguste Bouquet's lithograph published during the Napoleonic revival in the 1830s refers to the restoration of the statue of Napoleon in the Place Vendôme. Taken down during the Restoration, it was re-erected with a great deal of pomp and ceremony in July 1833. Its restoration was overseen by Louis Adolphe Thiers (1797-1877), a journalist, historian, and politician (Broadley, II, 273-274). Nationalistic, ambitious, and at times ruthless, Thiers dominated French politics from the 1830s to the 1870s. As Minister of the Interior in 1832, and again in 1834-36, he vigorously enforced law and order and violently quelled public demonstrations (*Historical Dictionary of France*, 1046-1052). He was in this respect similar to Napoleon.

75 Auguste Bouquet, *Mr. Thiers* from *La Caricature,* no. 144, August 8, 1833

Thiers figured frequently in the caricatures of the 1830s. Great French satirists like Daumier, Philipon, Grandville, and Bouquet mercilessly mocked the politician's diminutive, owl-like figure. In this print Bouquet ridicules Thiers's pretensions by placing him on the pedestal reserved for Napoleon. Mocking his stature through a pun on his name, the statue is marked "1/3." When it was published in the Paris journal *La Caricature*, an inscription indicated that Thiers's uniform was that of a civic policeman, not that of Napoleon, that his spyglass was an opera glass used to view the legs of dancers at the opera, and that the cannon-balls at his feet were merely pears. The image of the pear was used in caricatures of the 1830s to symbolize the detested "citizen king," Louis-Philippe (Universität Göttingen, 180-181, cat. no. 70).   A. J.

ABBREVIATIONS

B   Broadley, A. M. *Napoleon in Caricature 1795-1821.* The first part of the citation refers to a description of the caricature in Broadley and the second part refers to a conclusive list of titles and dates found in the appendix. Some caricatures are listed in the appendix but are not described in the text.

BE   *Bibliographie de l'Empire Français ou Journal de l'Imprimerie et de la Librairie*

BF   *Bibliographie de la France*

BM   British Museum, Department of Prints and Drawings. *Catalogue of Political and Personal Satires, Preserved in the Department of Prints and Drawings in the British Museum*

Cohn   Cohn, Albert M. *A Bibliographical Catalogue of the Printed Works Illustrated by George Cruikshank*

Coll. de Vinck   Bibliothèque Nationale, Département des estampes. *Un Siècle d'Histoire de France par l'estampe, 1770-1871: Collection de Vinck Inventaire analytique*

Grego   Grego, Joseph. *Rowlandson the Caricaturist*

Hennin   Bibliothèque Nationale, Département des estampes. *Collection Hennin, Inventaire de la Collection d'estampes relatives à l'histoire de France*

Inventaire 18e s   Bibliothèque Nationale, Département des estampes. *Inventaire du Fonds Français: Graveurs du dix-huitième siècle*

Inventaire 19e s   Bibliothèque Nationale, Département des estampes. *Inventaire du Fonds Français après 1800*

Wright   Wright, Thomas, and R. H. Evans. *Historical and Descriptive Account of the Caricatures of James Gillray*

BIBLIOGRAPHY

Adhémar, Jean. *Graphic Art of the Eighteenth and Nineteenth Century*. London: Thames and Hudson, 1964.

Angeloglou, Maggie. *A History of Make-Up*. London: Studio Vista, 1970.

Arsène, Alexandre. *L'Art du Rire et de la Caricature*. Paris: Librairies-Imprimeries, 1892.

Baltimore Museum of Arts. *Regency to Empire French Printmaking 1715-1814*. Baltimore: Baltimore Museum of Art, 1984.

Bates, William. *George Cruikshank: The Artist, the Humourist, and the Man*. Amsterdam: S. Emmering, 1972.

Bénézit, E. *Dictionnaire critique et documentaire des peintures, sculpteurs, dessinaterus et graveurs…*. Paris: Grund, 1976.

Beraldi, H. *Les Graveurs du XIXe siècle: Guide de l'amateur d'estampes modernes*. 12 vols. Paris: L. Conquet, 1885-92.

Berry, Mary. *Extracts from Journals and Correspondence of Miss Berry: From the Year 1783 to 1852*. London: Longmans, Green, 1865.

Bertuch, F. J., and G. M. Kraus, eds. *Journal des Luxus und der Moden*. Vols. 1-40, partial reprint. Hanau, Main: Muller & Kiepenheuer, 1786-1825.

Bibliographie de la France. Nendeln, Liechtenstein: reprinted with permission of Cercle de la Librairie Paris, Kraus reprint Ltd., 1966. Superceded the *Bibliographie de l'Empire Français ou Journal de l'Imprimerie et de la Librairie* as of issue no. 13 (May 1, 1814).

Bibliographie de l'Empire Français ou Journal de l'Imprimerie et de la Librairie. Nendeln, Liechtenstein: reprinted with permission of Cercle de la Librairie Paris, Kraus Reprint Ltd., 1966. Began print November 1, 1811, and was superceded by *Bibliographie de la France* as of issue no. 13 (May 1, 1814).

Bibliothèque Nationale, Départements des estampes. *Collection Hennin, Inventaire de la Collection d'estampes relatives à l'histoire de France*. Vols. 1-5. Paris: H. Menu, 1877-84.

———. *Inventaire du Fonds Français: Graveurs du dix-huitième siècle*. Edited by M. Roux. Paris: M. LeGarrec, 1930-1977.

———. *Inventaire du Fonds Français après 1800*. Edited by J. Laran. Paris: M. LeGarrec, 1930-85.

———. *Un Siècle d'Histoire de France par l'estampe, 1770-1871: Collection de Vinck Inventaire analytique*. Paris: Bibliothèque Nationale, 1970.

Bigelow, M. S. *Fashion in History: Apparel in the Western World*. Minneapolis: Burgess Pub. Co., 1970.

Black, J. Anderson. *A History of Fashion*. London: Orbis Pub., 1975.

Blagdon, F. W. *Paris as It Was and as It Is*. London: C. and R. Baldwin, 1803.

Boehn, Max von. *Modes and Manners of the Nineteenth Century as Represented in the Pictures and Engravings of the Time*. Philadelphia: J. B. Lippincott Company, 1932-36.

Boileau-Despréaux, Nicolas. *Le Lutrin: An Heroic Poem Written Originally in French by M. Boileau*. Los Angeles University of California: William Andrews Clark Memorial Library, 1967.

Bornemann, B. *La Caricature: Art et Manifeste, du 16e siècle à nos jours*. Genève: Skira, 1974.

Boucher, F. *Histoire de Costume en Occident de l'Antiquité à nos Jours*. Paris: Flammarion, 1965.

British Museum, Department of Prints and Drawings. *Catalogue of Political and Personal Satires, Preserved in the Department of Prints and Drawings in the British Museum*. 9 vols. Vols. IV and V compiled by F. G. Stephens, 1978; vols.

VI-IX compiled by M. D. George, 1978, 1942, 1947, 1949 respectively. London: Published for the Trustees of the British Museum by British Museum Publications.

Broadley, A.M. *Napoleon in Caricature 1795-1821*, 2 vols. London: Lane, 1911.

———. *The Journal of an English Chaplain in Paris during the Peace Negotiations of 1801-1802*. London: Chapman, 1913.

Brown University. Department of Art. *Caricature and Its Role in Graphic Satire*. Providence, R. I., 1971.

Champfleury. *Histoire de la Caricature sous la République, l'Empire et la Restauration*. Paris: E. Dentu, 1877.

Chapelle, Pierre de la. *Huit Siècles de Vie Britanique à Paris*. Paris: 1948.

Clerc, Catherine. *La Caricature contre Napoléon*. Paris: Éditions Promodis, 1985.

Cobban, Alfred. *History of Modern France from the First Empire to the Second Empire 1799-1871*. Vol. 2. 1965; rpt. Harmondsworth, Middlesex: Penguin Books, 1981.

Cohn, Albert M. *A Bibliographical Catalogue of the Printed Works Illustrated by George Cruikshank*. London: Longmans, Green, 1914.

Colas, René. *Bibliographie générale de Costume de la Mode*. Paris: R. Colas, 1933.

Connolly, Owen, ed. *Historical Dictionary of Napoleonic France 1799-1815*. Westport, Connecticut: Greenwood Press, 1985.

Corson, Richard. *Fashions in Hair: The First 5000 Years*. London: P. Owen, 1965.

———. *Fashions in Make-up: From Ancient to Modern Times*. London: P. Owen, 1972.

Cunnington, C. Willett. *Handbook of English Costume in the Eighteenth Century*. London: Faber and Faber, 1957.

———. *Handbook of English Costume in the*

Nineteenth Century. London: Faber and Faber, 1970.

Decaux, A., ed. *Dictionnaire de l'Histoire de France Perrin*. Paris: Librairie Academique Perrin, 1981.

Delteil, Loys. *Manuel de l'Amateur d'Estampes de XIX et XX Siècles 1801-1924*. Paris: Dorbonaine, 1925.

Dictionnaire de Paris. Paris: Libraire Larousse, 1964.

Duffy, Michael. *The Englishman and the Foreigner*. Cambridge: Chadwyck-Healey, 1986.

Fenaille, M. *L'Oeuvre gravé de P.-L. Debucourt*. Paris: D. Morgand, 1899.

Friedlaender, Walter. *David to Delacroix*. Cambridge: Harvard University Press, 1952.

Geipel, John. *The Cartoon: A Short History of Graphic Comedy and Satire*. South Brunswick: A. S. Barnes, 1972.

George, Mary Dorothy. *English Political Caricature to 1792: A Study of Opinion and Propaganda*. Oxford: Clarendon Press, 1959.

————. *English Political Caricature 1793-1832: A Study of Opinion and Propaganda*. Oxford: Clarendon Press, 1959.

————. *Hogarth to Cruikshank: Social Change in Graphic Satire*. London: Allen Lane, Penguin Press, 1967.

Ginsburg, Madeleine. *An Introduction to Fashion Illustration*. London: Victoria and Albert Museum, 1980.

————. *Four Hundred Years of Fashion*. London: Victoria and Albert Museum, 1984.

Gould, A. "La Gravure politique de Hogarth à Cruikshank" in *Revue de l'Art* 30 (1975): 39-49.

Grand-Carteret, John. *Les Moeurs et la Caricature en France*. Paris: Librairie Illustré, 1888.

Green, Frederick, ed. "Anglomaniacs and Francophiles." *Eighteenth-Century France: Six Essays*. New York: F. Ungar Pub. Co., 1964.

Grego, Joseph. *Rowlandson the Caricaturist*. 2 vols. London: Chatto and Windus, 1880.

Harvey, Sir Paul, ed. *Oxford Companion to French Literature*. Oxford: Clarendon Press, 1984.

Hayes, John. *Rowlandson Watercolours and Drawings*. London: Phaidon, 1972.

Herold, Christopher. *The Horizon Book of the Age of Napoleon*. New York: American Heritage Pub. Co., 1963.

Hill, Draper. *Mr. Gillray, the Caricaturist*. London: Phaidon Press, 1965.

————. *Fashionable Contrasts: Caricatures by James Gillray*. London, 1966.

————. *The Satirical Etchings of James Gillray*. New York: Dover Publications, 1976.

Hillairet, Jean. *Dictionnaire Historique des Rues de Paris*. Paris: Éditions de Minuit, 1963.

Holland, Vyvyan Beresford. *Hand-Coloured Fashion Plates 1770-1899*. London: Batsford, 1955.

Holtman, Robert B. *Napoleonic Revolution*. Philadelphia: Lippincott, 1967.

Jouve, Michel. *L'Age d'Or de la Caricature Anglaise*. Paris: Presses de la Fondation nationale des sciences politiques, 1983.

————. "L'image du sans-culotte dans la caricature politique anglaise: création d'un stéréotype pictural." *Gazette des Beaux Arts* (November 1978): 187-96.

Laing, Margaret. *Josephine and Napoleon*. London: Sidgwick and Jackson, 1973.

Langle, Vicomte Fleuriot de. "English Caricatures of Napoleon." *Connoisseur* 157 no. 633 (November 1964), 181, no. 14, 177-181.

Larousse, Pierre, ed. *Grand Dictionnaire Universel du XIXe Siècle*. Paris: Vᵛᵉ P. Larousse & Cⁱᵉ, Imprimeurs – Éditeurs, 1865-90.

Laver, James. *Taste and Fashion from the French Revolution to the Present Day*. London: Harrap, 1937.

————. *Concise History of Costume*. London: Thames and Hudson, 1969.

Le Blanc, Charles. *Manuel de l'Amateur d'Estampes, contenant un dictionnaire des graveurs de toutes les nations....* Amsterdam:

G. W. Hissink, 1970.

Lyons, Martyn. *France Under the Directory*. London: Cambridge University Press, 1975.

Markham, F. M. H. *Napoleon and the Awakening of Europe*. London: English Universities Press, 1954.

Marlet, Jean-Henri. *Tableaux de Paris*. Paris, Genève: Slatkine, 1979.

Maurice, A. B., and F. T. Cooper. *The History of the Nineteenth Century in Caricature*. New York: Dodd, Mead, 1904.

Maxwell, Constantia. *The English Traveller in France 1698-1815*. London: Routledge, 1932.

Mercier, Louis Sebastien. *The Picture of Paris Before and After the Revolution*. London: Routledge, 1929.

————. *The Waiting City: Paris 1782-88*. London: G. G. Harrap and Co. Ltd., 1933.

Musée Carnevalet. *L'Art de l'Estampe et la Révolution*. Alençon: F. D. Imprimerie Alençonnaise, 1980.

Newman, Edgar Leon, ed. *Historical Dictionary of France from the Restoration to the Second Empire*. Westport, Connecticut: Greenwood Press, 1987.

Palmer, Alan W. *Encyclopaedia of Napoleon's Europe*. London: Weidenfeld and Nicolson, 1984.

Paston, George [Emily Morse Symonds]. *Social Caricature in the Eighteenth Century*. London: Methuen, 1905.

Paulson, Ronald. *Rowlandson: A New Interpretation*. London: Studio Vista, 1972.

Payne, Blanche. *History of Costume From the Ancient Egyptians to the Twentieth Century*. New York: Harper and Row, 1965.

Petit Larousse Illustré. Paris: Librairie Larousse, 1981.

Rix, Brenda. *Our Old Friend Rolly: Watercolours, Prints, and Book Illustrations by Thomas Rowlandson*. Toronto: Art Gallery of Ontario, 1987.

Robiquet, Jean. *Daily Life in France under*

Napoleon. London: Allen and Unwin, 1962.

Rudé, George. *Revolutionary Europe 1783-1815*. 1964; rpt. London: Fontana Paperbacks, 1985.

Schnapper, Antoine. *David*. New York: Alpine Fine Arts, 1982.

Scott, John. *A Visit to Paris in 1814*. London: Printed for Longmans, 1815.

Scott, Samuel F., and Barry Rothaus, eds. *Historical Dictionary of the French Revolution 1789-1799*. Westport, Connecticut: Greenwood Press, 1985.

Scribe, Eugène. *Oeuvres Complètes de Eugène Scribe*. Vols II, III. Paris: E. Dentu, 1874-85.

Simond, Charles, ed. *Paris de 1800 à 1900 d'après les Estampes et les Memoires du temps*. Tomes I, II. Paris: Plon, 1900-1901.

Stephen, L., and S. Lee, eds. *Dictionary of National Biography*. 1917; rpt. London: Oxford University Press, 1963-64.

Streicher, L. H. "On a Theory of Political Caricature." *Comparative Studies in Society and History*. 9:4 (1967): 427-445.

Twyman, Michael. *Lithography 1800-1850*. London: Oxford University Press, 1970.

Universität Göttingen. *La Caricature: Bildsatire in Frankreich 1830-1835 aus der Sammlung von Kritter*. Göttingen: Erich Goltze GmbH & Co. K. G., 1980.

Victoria and Albert Museum. *English Caricature 1620 to the Present: Caricaturists and Satirists, Their Art, Their Purpose and Influence*. London: Victoria and Albert Museum, 1984.

Wardroper, John. *The Caricatures of George Cruikshank*. London: G. Fraser, 1977.

Webb, R. K., ed. *Modern England: From the Eighteenth Century to the Present*. 1968; rpt. New York: Dodd, Mead, 1980.

Wechsler, Judith. *A Human Comedy: Physiognomy and Caricature in Nineteenth-Century Paris*. London: Thames and Hudson, 1982.

Weigert, Roger Armand. *Galerie des Modes et Costumes Français*. Paris: Rombaldi, 1956.

Wilcox, R. T. *The Dictionary of Costume*. New York: Scribner, 1969.

Wright, Thomas, and R. H. Evans. *Historical and Descriptive Account of the Caricatures of James Gillray*. London: B. Blom, 1968.

Text set in Simoncini Garamond

Heads set in Bauer Bodoni Black

Printed on Media print Satin